Driving Institute of America presents

The Teen Driver's Bible

The Parents' Guide for Supporting Their Teen's Critical First Phase of Driving

Manuel "Manny" Moncivais Jr.

Driving Institute of America

ISBN 978-1-64569-011-5 (paperback)
ISBN 978-1-64569-012-2 (digital)

Christian Faith Publishing, Inc.
832 Park Avenue
Meadville, PA 16335
www.christianfaithpublishing.com

Illustrations by Lisa Garcia Moncivais

Printed in the United States of America

I dedicate this to many: first God, Dad, and Mom, for your unconditional love. You showed so much humility, and that love was always most important. Mom, we finally got it done!

To Diana, for saying, "Yes, let's go" a few times, which started our journey, and for being a great wife and mother to Marc and Noah, and for your amazing work ethic. RIP.

To Marc and Noah for making a parent proud, thankful for being you, and for being strong when it counted.

To my wife Lisa, for your amazing love, patience, and support in this endeavor. You came at the right time. God answered my prayer.

To my sisters, Dora M. Garcia and Vivi Rini, for being my cheerleaders, and Dora, the best nurse ever!

To Tia Angie, for sending all the clippings keeping me motivated with the passion to get this important knowledge out. What a blessing.

To Adrian Eli Moncivais for inspiring me to finish this project.

To Stephanie Conway Gauthreaux for the original flip charts.

Thanks to Dr. Robert Cline for putting me back together.

To the Moncivais, Medina, Garcia, and Alderete families for all their prayers and support, love you all!

To the following individuals who supported me from the beginning of this career: John V. Griffin, Jim Stewart, Al Hammett, Ron S. Texeira, Larry Long, John Roberts, Cliff Hardt, Ted Merida, Steve Smith, Mike Metzger, Jeff Mazur, Joe Joyce, Cesar Valenzuela, Randy Weisbrod, Ralph Spitsnaugle, Ken J. Rael, Joe Fife, Howard Morgan, and Robert Bonilla. We made it happen and made it fun!

Finally, to all whom I worked with at FedEx and UPS during my career and all those who still do it every day! I salute you! Safe driving!

And especially dedicated to the memory of all those we have lost in vehicle accidents. RIP.

For the waywardness of the simple will kill them, and the complacency of fools will destroy them; but whoever listens to me will live in safety, and be at ease without fear of harm.

Proverbs 1:32–33

Driving Institute of America's curriculum is based on preventative, fundamental focus concepts and is not liable for any action or inaction of anyone who is driving in various situations that may arise. As a person behind the wheel, your goal is to follow all measures that will help prevent any accident ahead of time, by being focused, proactive, and defensive based on this preventative curriculum. There will be the possibilities where an accident is completely not preventable.

Although I feel every word in this training is important, bold print and underlines will be used for curriculum emphasis, accident scenario descriptions, accident prevention solutions, and the important, fundamental focus concepts being taught.

Contents

Introduction

We have some major problems on our roads today! The past thirty years, we have averaged 120 fatalities every single day along with an average of 6.000 injuries daily due to vehicle accidents. This equals over 1.3 million fatalities and another 65.7 million injuries! <u>According to National Safety Council's Accident Facts, from 2000 to 2018, there have been 768,828 fatalities (73,545 teens) and over 39.4 million injuries; this easily could have been you or me!</u> Some of these injuries were very serious: lost limbs, serious brain injuries, or permanent paralysis requiring months or years of rehabilitation and hospitalization. <u>Simply put, our present driver training is not working!</u>

Now, the question I ask is, How many of these drivers would have said, "I'm a good driver?" Yes, almost all of them! Then what happened? The answers are very simple; they were not that good, based on two major root causes which we will cover in this hook. I strongly and wholeheartedly believe this curriculum will change the way you drive forever! I feel very strongly that 90 percent of these fatalities were preventable.

The present statistics are due to two major root causes. The first of the two root causes is lack of proper knowledge, due to a general introductory curriculum and not a fundamentals-based focus-concept training with accident situations. In 2016, 2017, and 2018, we had over 40,000 fatalities each year, the most in nine (9) years! **THIS IS UNACCEPTABLE!** <u>It is time to retrain every person driving a vehicle!</u> And second is bad driving habits (behavioral) drivers have developed along the way. Regarding the bad behavioral habits, we will focus on the two main bad habits: (1) Distractions and (2) Speeding. Not being well rested is another huge factor causing many serious accidents, and we will address this also.

We all would agree that knowledge is power, but <u>in this book, we will show you how knowledge is prevention!</u> What you will learn will be a more "Xs and Os" type of training with DIA's focus concepts, along with accident-possibility situations with diagrams and prevention steps. These focus concepts will become second-nature habits as you drive.

We are creatures of habit, so if you have a bad habit of rolling through stop signs, this habit will eventually catch up to you. Trust me on this. You must correct this habit immediately! I have put a lot of work and thought into every module in this curriculum, and I can assure you will become a much safer driver if you execute what is taught. Some modules are short, and some are more detailed; but once you have completed them, you are on your way to improving your new disciplined driving skills. You will never drive the same again! <u>I do not like using the word I much, although it is used in this book because this is how exactly I try to drive when on our highways.</u>

You will have a new knowledge and mindset regarding how you perceive driving, your attitude toward how you drive will change, you will be more disciplined, and you will also eliminate the most dangerous word, COMPLACENCY!

It is much easier to get you to visit your dentist than to go to a Driver Safety class? Why? Pain! The only way you will attend a Driver Safety class is when you receive a citation and you take the driver course to remove the citation off your record. Your first comment after taking the training would be "This was a good refresher course. I'm glad I went through this." <u>This book is not a refresher course! Instead, this is a SURVIVAL course teaching you how to survive in THE MOST DANGEROUS PLACE IN THE WORLD—THE PUBLIC HIGHWAYS!</u>

After reading this book and reviewing all the focus concepts and the diagrams, you will start FOCUSING ON BEING 100 PERCENT IN CONTROL FROM POINT A TO POINT B ON EVERY DRIVING MISSION!

You will learn several fundamental survival habits such as this one. **You are stopped on a rural two-lane major highway at an uncontrolled intersection preparing to make a left turn. You have your wheels turned, prior to making the turn, as you wait for the oncoming traffic to pass. Suddenly a vehicle strikes you from behind! With your wheels turned, you will automatically be pushed into the path of the oncoming traffic! This has been the root cause of many serious and deadly accidents! This becomes a head-on collision, but I also classify this as a freak accident.** This is one example of a driver who thought he or she was a good driver but found out the hard way, in one split second of a fundamental habit, you should always remember to execute. When stopped in traffic preparing to make a left turn, **the focus concept is, never ever turn your wheels until you are ready to execute the turn! Make this a new habit!** Remember, our mission is your survival on the highways!

I was talking to a friend one evening; we reviewed three different diagrams regarding serious types of accident possibilities on the roads she drove every day, and what caused them. After our discussion she said, "You just saved my life three different ways!" She understood what I had taught her. She had never been taught this anywhere, and she would now execute these new habits. This is my goal with this book: to communicate these possibly life-saving concepts to every driver in the world!

I have put together this training after working over thirty-nine years in the transportation field, with 200,000 miles of observing delivery couriers, and driving over 500,000 miles myself. I am determined to share and spread this new knowledge when driving, focused on serious-accident prevention. The above example is just one situation that Driving Institute of America (DIA) teaches in its curriculum, along with other life-saving philosophies not taught by anyone else today.

HERE'S THE DEAL: SIMPLY PUT, IF YOU DRIVE A VEHICLE, YOU NEED THIS BOOK. You will be shown the correct and incorrect steps in several accident situations in order that you are not a vulnerable accident victim. These diagrams will be easy to understand, read them completely, and make them consistent, disciplined habits. DIA's definition of a DIA-Certified Teen Driver is "ONE WHO IS 100 PERCENT DISCIPLINED IN FOLLOWING AND EXECUTING ALL THE DIA FOCUS CONCEPTS ON EVERY DRIVING MISSION EVERY DAY FOR THE REST OF THEIR LIFE." WE ARE STILL A WORK IN PROGRESS.

Driving Institute of America's definition of a DIA-Certified Teen Driver also has several individual definitions, disciplines, and habits, which will become your new disciplined habits. You will find these nineteen elements in The DIA-Certified Teen Driver vs. The Teen Driver training module.

Our mission is to make you a DIA-Certified Teen Driver! DIA. also wants you to "drive like a surgeon." This is your goal: driving like a surgeon who is focused 100 percent on the patient, performing a delicate operation until it is 100 percent complete; you too must focus 100 percent on your driving mission from the beginning (point A) until arriving at your destination (point B).

This training is designed to be simple, although at times you need to reread to understand the focus concept, habit, or situation. You will learn how to detect and expect possible accident situations ahead of time. Your goal is to be a proactive driver versus a reactive driver at all times.

This curriculum includes the DIA-Certified Teen Driver Certification and Pledge, for you to complete along with the DIA DangerZones Roadtest Knowledge Review. Once you complete the DIA-Certified Teen Driver Certification and Pledge, you may contact www.dia7.net or Christian Faith Publishing link for insurance companies offering premium discounts for you completing the DIA course.

This curriculum is not part of any state program; instead, it is an additional, supplemental preventative training program to help you survive on our nation's highways! **DIA wants you to share this information with all your loved ones. My goal is to create the most knowledgeable, non-complacent, and safest drivers in the world—one driver at a time!** Another objective is to Serious Accident-Proof' you when you get behind the wheel. DIA's other goal is to reach TARGET ZERO! With ZERO fatalities in the USA one day! SAFE DRIVING.

You are about to enter the most dangerous place in the world—

The Public Highways!

United States Fatalities

Improved safety in vehicles (airbags, ABS) has led to higher injuries versus deaths.

Year	Fatalities	Year	Fatalities
2018	40,000	1900	36
2017	40,231	1907	581
2016	40,327	1909	1174
2015	32,092	1918	10,390
2014	32,675	1966–1973	Over 50,000/yr.
2013	32,788	1972	54,589

A total of 768,828 fatalities between 2000 and 2018
And over 39.4 million injuries! (From National Safety Council's Accident Facts)

The DIA® Mission

The DIA® Mission is to make you a <u>DIA-Certified Teen Driver</u> vs. a good driver, by

1. Giving you a "New Knowledge" of <u>accident-possibility</u> situations caused by you or by others.
2. Giving you a New Knowledge for <u>Proactive prevention</u> of all possible accidents, to become a Proactive vs. Reactive driver. **Reactive is too late!**
3. Giving you a New Knowledge that eliminates any bad driving habits and develops new driving skills to execute the Focus Concepts on every driving mission.

The Two Major Root Causes of Accidents

ROOT CAUSE #1

The driver's education curriculum taught in high school was too general, not simple, or fundamentals-based driven. Different accident situations and how they could be prevented were not a focus, therefore not part of the curriculum. To succeed in sports, you must learn the fundamentals of each sport; the same is true with driving. Even those of us who have been driving over thirty, forty, fifty years received this same type of training. There have been some improvements, but I feel the terrible fatality and injury statistics reflect we need a much better preventative curriculum.

ROOT CAUSE #2

The second root cause is behavioral: just plain bad driving habits! Here is an example of one of the most important disciplines that is a major factor in many accidents. A person who is consistently departing late immediately becomes like a ticking time bomb! This person becomes a very aggressive driver! An aggressive driver becomes a less defensive driver, and the accident possibilities increase dramatically! This driver is usually the primary person causing an accident.

If this sounds like you, we will start now to correct this habit when you drive by following DIA's "1520 Rule." This simply means being disciplined by departing in sufficient time so that you arrive at your destination 15–20 minutes ahead of time. Make this a disciplined habit, and you will see how less stressful, and safer, your driving mission will become. You allow extra time for others pulling out; it eliminates you tailgating, running red lights, making hasty pullouts, speeding, unplanned abrupt lane changes, or losing control! This simple concept will improve your driving behavior immensely.

When we first start driving, there are two very critical phases that we enter as drivers. These are the first ten years of driving; the first phase is from 16 to 20 years. This most critical phase requires the utmost focus and discipline as a new driver on the road. The accident statistics may get worse before they improve because of our large aging society. The 74 million baby boomers are getting older, and many still driving on the roads. With many more elderly drivers on the road, the possibilities of these drivers crossing the centerline, pulling out at intersections carelessly, or losing control will become more prevalent.

When reading your local paper or local news, look how many times you see, or hear "the driver crossed the centerline!" We also now have a generation exceeding the baby boomer generation, with the millennial generation totaling seventy-six million people! These two segments of society are high in numbers regarding accidents! As we have heard before, it takes twenty-one days to make a habit a consistent habit. We will give you the knowledge and behavioral habits that you need to change. Remember, this is a fundamental focus-concept driver training curriculum.

Two Root Causes for Accident Statistics

1. **Drivers' Education**—Too general, not fundamentally focus-concept based
2. **Driver Behavior**—Bad habits

Two Major Driver Behavior Root Causes

1. <u>**Distractions**</u>—looking away from the road, on cell phone, texting, or looking at passengers "while the wheels are rolling!"
2. <u>**Speeding**</u>

It's Not Preventable—Oh Yes, It Is!

During my tenure in the transportation industry, when discussing accidents with friends or relatives, it was extremely difficult for them to accept responsibility that the accident was preventable.

Although I agree there are some accidents (approximately 10–20 percent) that are completely non-preventable, these are rare. I could look where the vehicle was damaged and if it was in the front of the vehicle, the likelihood of it being preventable was higher.

You will learn the focus concept to prevent you from getting rear-ended by another vehicle when you are stopped in traffic. Most people would say this type of accident cannot be prevented, but it surely can be prevented. We will show you how you can prevent being rear-ended in this training.

Now, let us look at the DIA focus concept when approaching an intersection with a green light. Your new DIA focus concept is "A green light will not mean go only. Instead, it will mean "Go—proceeding with caution!"

When you approach a green light with the perception of "go", you will most likely drive assuming the cross traffic is going to stop. Therefore, you are just cruising along happy-go-lucky, then crash!

When you approach the green light with the "Go—proceeding with caution" mindset, you will approach the intersection differently. Once you see the cross traffic approaching, you will proceed at the proper speed to check and ensure the other vehicle is indeed slowing down. Only then can you proceed safely through the intersection. If you see the vehicle not slowing down, you make the decision to slow down prior to entering the intersection and prevent a serious accident. Available visibility also determines how you approach each individual intersection.

This also applies to you when you are the first vehicle stopped at a red light and the light changes to green; you want to hesitate, clear all sides properly, and make sure the cross-traffic stops! Go—proceeding with caution! I never want to be the vehicle being hit by someone who runs a red light! Many of these red-light runners have been drivers under the influence also.

The National Safety Council's statistics rated intersection accidents as being the cause of 43 percent of all fatalities in vehicle accidents, although this is changing drastically because of the lost-control type of accidents climbing at a fast rate. The major causes of lost-control type of accidents soaring are various distractions and speeding. More drivers are using cell phones, texting, using laptops, eating, falling articles, changing radio/CD/MP3 players, pets in vehicle, checking GPS, reading books, and dozing off all while the wheels are rolling!

Teen Driver's Critical First Phase Facts

FACT: <u>Crash rate for seventeen- to nineteen-year-olds per mile driven is four times a higher risk.</u>

FACT: <u>Crash rate for sixteen-year-olds per mile driven is eight times a higher risk!</u>

FACT: <u>From 2000 to 2017, over 73,545 teens ages sixteen to nineteen died in the US from auto crashes.</u>

FACT: Two out of every three (66 percent) fatalities were males, 34 percent were females.

FACT: In these accidents, the teen driver was more likely at fault.

FACT: Teenagers do most driving at night.

FACT: 20 percent of fatalities from 9:00 p.m. to midnight

FACT: 23 percent of fatalities from midnight to 6:00 a.m.

FACT: Teens are involved in more single-vehicle accidents (lost control) than other drivers.

FACT: Teens are inexperienced, lack proper detection skills, are easily distracted, and unable to maintain proper speed on a consistent basis.

FACT: The best practices are to limit and minimize the teen's driving exposure. This is especially true for sixteen-year-olds. If you have a teen who is hyper and hasty, the odds are they will tend to speed or become easily distracted. A true recipe for disaster is a sixteen-year-old running late to school, or anywhere!

FACT: 15 percent of sixteen- to seventeen-year-old males had BAC 0.08 or higher.

FACT: 10 percent of sixteen- to seventeen-year-old females had BAC 0.08 or higher—must eliminate this!

As a parent, or guardian, you must invest sufficient time in training your teen. DIA's curriculum is intended as an added support to the state driver's education training focused on accident prevention.

Teen Accident Statistics Review

➤ From 2000 to 2017, 73,545 teen fatalities.
➤ **Crash rate for seventeen- to nineteen-year-olds is four times higher, versus for sixteen-year-olds, which is eight times higher!**
➤ Teens are involved in more single-vehicle accidents (Root causes: Distractions and Speeding).
➤ DIA's suggested driving plan is a supplemental addition to the state program and is designed to help you support your teen.

Let's Cut To The Chase! (For Parents)

All right, this is very important for every parent to understand immediately! Parents spend thousands of dollars on their teen's extracurricular activities: dancing, golf, piano, or tennis lessons. Yet when it comes to defensive-driver training, there is a very small investment made for their teens' most important need: their survival on the public highways. What is more important? Their survival, of course! An important step is that you analyze your teen's maturity and emotional level and determine the correct age to start their initial driver training. Is your teen very hyper or hasty? This is not a good sign. This is a signal of immaturity that will most likely be reflected also on the road. Together, our mission is to help your teen survive this critical first phase of driving. Don't rush it!

Your mission objectives in this training are as follows:

1. Read the training modules together with your teen and learn all the focus concepts.
2. Be a 100-percenter in all the focus concepts yourself and set a great example.
3. Never cease communicating all of the focus concepts and safety tips.
4. Most important, devote sufficient time with "The First Five Routes" and DangerZones road tests as mentioned in the First Five Routes module.
5. Complete DIA-Certified Teen Driver's DangerZone Roadtest Knowledge Review (TM pending), and DIA-Certified Teen Driver Certification and Pledge (TM pending).
6. Follow up with DangerZone Roadtests (TM pending) periodically.
7. Again, you must invest time with your teen, or have a professional complete this booklet and make them "a DIA-Certified Teen Driver!"
8. Go to the DIA website (www.dia7.net) and refer to the insurance companies giving discounts based on completing this curriculum. Our goal is to give you the absolute best training available anywhere today!

Parents: Let's Cut to the Chase Review

➤ Your mission is to support your teen to survive their critical first phase of driving.

➤ Invest sufficient and quality time with your teen.

➤ Start on road training at ages 16 1/2 to 17.

➤ Follow the suggested DIA training plan.

➤ Analyze your teen's maturity level! Are they hyper? Responsible?

➤ Set the example from what you learn in the DIA curriculum as you will become the secondary trainer.

Let's Cut To The Chase! (For Teen Drivers)

You are about to start a very critical phase in your life! It is the first phase of driving a motor vehicle. I myself went through this phase and can only tell you it is a miracle I made it this far. As teens, we do things to impress our friends. I remember driving 137 miles an hour once—not smart, to put it mildly. The frontal lobe of our brain is not completely developed until we reach our mid-twenties. This creates indecision, taking chances, and there is a higher risk of being in an accident that could be fatal.

My career took me into the transportation field (over thirty-nine years), and it gave me a new awareness of respecting the highway. I observed and trained drivers accumulating over 200,000 miles and drove over 500,000 miles during my career. I still consider myself a work in progress and have eliminated the word complacency from my vocabulary. It is a DANGEROUS WORD! I saw a sign once that read "YOU ARE ABOUT TO ENTER THE MOST DANGEROUS PLACE IN THE WORLD—THE PUBLIC HIGHWAYS. DRIVE SAFELY!" I never forgot this, and I want you to never forget this either. You want to remember this every time you get behind the wheel. This curriculum is an additional, supplemental training to help support you during your first phase of driving (age 16–20).

When we look at the root causes of almost all accidents, it boils down to these two: (1) distractions and (2) speeding. Here's the deal. If there is one thing I want you to remember, it is this: YOU MUST BE DISCIPLINED IN THE 1520 RULE, which means you will always plan on arriving at your destination a minimum of 15–20 minutes ahead of schedule. We will discuss this focus concept more in your training. It is extremely important for you to follow this and eliminate the SPEED FACTOR. To me, it is the most important focus concept.

A teen running late to their destination highly increases the possibilities of being in an accident!

The lost-control type of accident is the #1 serious type of accident involving teens, and the solution is simply to eliminate distractions, especially TEXTING and speeding, which we will also cover in your DIA training.

Our society is getting older, and medical conditions may cause an oncoming driver to cross the centerline. As a new teen driver, will you be proactive or reactive? Being reactive in this situation usually results in a HEAD-ON collision! I want you to be proactive! When I make the decision to drive in the left lane (on a four-lane undivided hwy), I try to have an opening into the right lane (by being STAGGERED/OFFSET) as much as possible and being proactive expecting an oncoming car to possibly cross the centerline! This book will be different from what you had in Driver's Ed because it will discuss and review lane strategies, fundamentals, and teach you different accident scenarios. Most importantly, what DIA calls focus concepts that are not too general or complex but instead simple, short phrases will be taught. Being disciplined is the key for your continued progress during your first phase of driving.

My dream is for every parent and teen who reads and understands all the DIA FOCUS CONCEPTS to live by them. And as DIA says, the definition of a DIA-Certified Teen Driver is "ONE WHO IS 100

PERCENT DISCIPLINED IN FOLLOWING AND EXECUTING ALL THE DIA FOCUS CONCEPTS EVERY DAY FOR THE REST OF THEIR LIFE!" WE ARE STILL A WORK IN PROGRESS. NEVER BECOME COMPLACENT!

Although you will see some repetition in this curriculum, it is intentional for improving the retention of all the DIA focus concepts.

Once you complete the DIA-Certified Teen Driver Certification and Pledge and the DIA-Certified Teen Driver DangerZone Roadtest Knowledge and Review, you can focus on executing what you have learned. LET'S DRIVE TO SURVIVE! SAFE DRIVING.

Teens: Let's Cut to the Chase Review

➢ You are responsible for yourself, your family, and your community all the time when driving behind the wheel.
➢ Your life can change in one split second!
➢ Driving is a privilege, not a right.
➢ The lost-control type of accidents is the #1 teen killer!
➢ Be a "Disciplined 1520" driver! ELIMINATE SPEEDING.
➢ Eliminate distractions: NO TEXTING!
➢ What you learn here make disciplined habits.
➢ Be a 100-percenter!

Your Teen's First-Year Driving Plan

DIA recommends this additional driver training for your teen. If you have someone else training your teen, they need to read this curriculum completely before they begin the training. DIA suggests holding off your sixteen-year-old driver until six months after their sixteenth birthday. Starting your teen at seventeen would be a better plan. There are several states that do not let sixteen-year-olds drive at all until age seventeen. Again, don't rush it! Many teens are waiting longer.

The first step we suggest you follow with your teen is familiarity with the vehicle they are going to drive. The following topics and training should be conducted in a large parking lot, normally on a Saturday, or Sunday afternoon. Find a large area near a church or school, with no traffic. Note: Scan the parking lot completely for barricades, curbs, fences, or light poles before you begin the training session. You will begin training by giving a commentary regarding all the instrumentation of the vehicle. Eliminating all in-vehicle distractions is of utmost importance here.

Instrumentation

It is extremely critical your teen knows exactly where and how each part of the instrumentation works. You want to prevent your teen from being distracted by looking for the wipers or trying to set cruise on while the wheels are rolling! Your teen, once being completely familiar with all the instrumentation, should avoid any in-vehicle distractions. Have your teen give you a complete commentary regarding all the instrumentation in their vehicle. Do this completely a minimum of ten times each, or more. If you are not satisfied they are completely familiar with all items, keep doing it! Although, it may sound redundant, repetition is the key here. Practice, practice, practice, and follow up periodically.

DIA Pre-Drive Check and Setup Routine

Distractions are large reasons for teen vehicle accidents. The lost-control type of accident is the #1 teen killer! DIA's Pre-Drive Check and Setup Routine focuses on eliminating these in-vehicle distractions. With all of today's gadgets, cell phones, tablets, iPods, MP3 players, DIA's focus concept here is to have all items secured properly in an area to avoid falling off dash, and the teen having to look for them. Have radio/CD/MP3 player set on station before your wheels begin to roll! Secure all personal articles and avoid looking down for them once the wheels are rolling! DIA Focus Concept: keep a clean, organized, secured dash and console at all times! When there are passengers in vehicle, avoid looking at them as you talk—focus on the road.

Mirror Adjustment

Did you know most drivers do not have their side mirrors adjusted properly? If they are set too far inward, they enlarge their blind spot. You do not want this! Check your mirror adjustment by keeping your head straight, then turn head slightly toward each mirror. If you see too much of your vehicle, they are overlapping with the middle mirror, and you need to adjust mirrors <u>out</u> more. You now have minimized your blind-spot areas, and you must use all three mirrors together to get maximum rear visibility. This is important when making lane changes. Remember, <u>use all three mirrors together!</u> Have your teen set their mirrors according to this focus concept.

Brake, Gas, and Steering

We have seen this in our newspaper or newscast: either an elderly or a teen driver stepped on the gas instead of the brake! Well, during these initial training sessions in the parking lot, invest sufficient time with your teen stopping and accelerating. Again, repetition is the important step here.

With vehicle turned off, have teen step on brake and gas pedal at your commands. Repeat this as much as you feel is necessary. Start vehicle; next, work slowly on smooth stops and, little by little, quicker stops. Continue this process until you feel they have mastered the stop-and-go maneuver consistently. Next, you want to work on your teen steering at your commands. Note: Before you start the steering process, look out for the possibility of other vehicles approaching in the parking lot.

The next step now, once you have invested sufficient time and feel that your teen is ready, is to plan the First Five Driving Routes.

The Sixteen-Year-Old's Driving Plan

As mentioned earlier, a sixteen-year-old's accident risks are eight times higher than all other drivers on the road! Therefore, DIA suggests this driving plan for your sixteen-year-old. Identify the First Five Driving Routes your teen will be driving on a consistent basis. For example, from home to school, from school to work/soccer practice, from home to grocery/pharmacy and back home. <u>Once you have determined these as the first five routes, the parent/guardian will be the only one to drive these routes during the first six months (minimum). The teen would start at 16 1/2 to drive these same routes, although DIA recommends parent/guardian start driving at 16 1/2 on these first five routes, then teen begins driving them at age 17.</u> You will <u>analyze all the DangerZones of each route; "The 12 DangerZones" will be given to you along with other modules of this workbook.</u> As you drive, you will give a commentary regarding what you are doing. Teen will do a commentary also when they drive. Commentary example: "I am approaching the red light and I am automatically checking mirrors and protecting the space in front of me by controlling the vehicle behind me."

After the first six months of you driving these First Five Driving Routes, then your seventeen-year-old can begin to drive these same routes with you in the vehicle. They should also give you a commentary of all the focus concepts taught in the DIA curriculum. Remember, the two main root causes of accidents stem from distractions and speeding, so as the trainer, ensure proper speed control is maintained at all times, and your teen is 100 percent focused on the road. Focus on discussing and reviewing all highway warning and speed limits ahead of time on each route.

*If your teen looks at you while the wheels are rolling, immediately tell them to focus on the road and not look at you! They can talk as they look at what is happening on the road, instead of looking at you. Again, DIA's focus concept is, when the wheels are rolling, you can't be looking down, TEXTING, or looking at any passengers!

Other DangerZones are as follows:

Curves and hills, which reduce visibility (teen reduces speed accordingly) **Blind spots such as buildings and trees** also reduce visibility. Lanes that merge (three lanes become two)—know where these are. Learn all **lane endings** on all five routes driven. Also develop a consistent strategic lane driving plan for each of the first five routes. Having to make left turns at uncontrolled intersections (check mirrors and control the traffic behind you in advance) can be dangerous. Very important: try to avoid having to make **left turns at uncontrolled intersections**. **Parked cars in residential areas**—check for drivers in vehicles and the wheels turned out, also checking closely for children hidden in front or between these parked cars. Adjust speed on roads where wildlife exists (heavily wooded areas), along with major intersections with **on-ramps and off-ramps**. Be prepared for other drivers making abrupt lane changes. DIA focus concept is to blend in, adjust speed accordingly.

Preplan all your lane changes, especially on high-speed highways! Avoid following trucks with heavy machinery, landscape materials, and equipment. Warning signs: Be aware and knowledgeable of all the warning signs of each of the First Five Routes.

Refer to "The 12 DangerZones," "DangerZone Roadtests," and "DangerZones Roadtest Knowledge and Review" modules.

The First Year: Your Teen's Driving Plan Review

➢ Start training at 16 1/2 to 17 years of age.
➢ Find practice area and time.
➢ For example: large parking lots, like at a church or high school, and on a Saturday or Sunday afternoon.
➢ Complete understanding and knowledge of vehicle's instrumentation.
➢ Learn the DIA Proper Mirror Adjustment.
➢ Repetitively practice on brake and gas pedals (stopping and accelerating).

The First Five Routes: Analyze Your Area and DangerZones

This is a continuation of DIA's sixteen-year-old's driving plan. This phase is critical for you both to understand and follow. As defined earlier, you will designate the First Five Routes your teen will be driving on a consistent basis. These are the only routes that will be driven by your teen during the first six months of driving. <u>Again, for the first six months after age sixteen (DIA's recommendation), you, the parent, will be the initial driver of these routes.</u> We need to make these first five routes the most practical. Examples are as follows:

1. From Home to School and Return
2. From School to Work and Return Home
3. From Home to Work and Return (What is different on return trip?)
4. From Home to Grocery Store and Return
5. From Home to Pharmacy and Return

Analyze each route option

1.   <u>This is very important: look for alternate routes for each of the five routes, analyze them to see which is a safer route to each destination. If one route has much more traffic, higher speed limits, requires more left turns, but there is another route to the same destination that goes through a residential area with less traffic, you would want to choose the residential route. It is, simply put, the safer route for your teen, if you will. You want to minimize left turns as much as possible, especially at uncontrolled intersections. Going to controlled intersections where there is a light is the preferred option for your new teen driver, and for you.</u> I have an intersection near my home where taking the uncontrolled intersection is usually a more stressful experience with more accident possibilities, so I go one more block to the traffic light. <u>"Left turns at controlled intersections are safer" is the focus concept here.</u>
2. Next, you want to analyze the area and the route for the DangerZones involved.

Analyze the area

- In the block where you live, do you have toddlers living close by? This is critical, for each time you back out of the driveway, you want to ensure the area behind you is clear. You must make it a disciplined habit that anytime you or your teen backs up, <u>you physically check the rear of the vehicle,</u> back up slowly and promptly after checking. Also, <u>make it a habit to tap your horn a couple of</u>

times prior to backing up. Tapping the horn will always be a habit when backing out, especially in parking lots—got it? Good!

- **When driving down the block, are there curves and hills?** Again, remember this: curves and hills will reduce your visibility; therefore, you simply reduce your speed. You have no idea what is around the curve or over the hill! Focus concept: Curves and hills = reduced visibility, so simply reduce your speed.

- **Are there a lot of buildings, blind intersections, or trees?** Buildings and trees also reduce your visibility; therefore, you must reduce speed accordingly. If you are disciplined in the 1520 Rule, you should be driving the speed limit already.

- **Is there a lot of wildlife in the area?** With many people moving out to the suburbs and country, you may have areas filled with deer. This is another area where you need to maintain safe speeds. I have an area where deer are plentiful on one route lined with many trees, so I choose an alternate route and avoid this area altogether. When driving on these heavily wooded roads at night (usually two-lane roads), I drive 5–10 miles slower than the speed limit (Focus concept: Minus 5, Minus 10 MPH). The same as if it were raining, you would not drive the speed limit on the wet, slick roads.

- **Are there many senior citizens living in the area?** You need to be aware of this also, for you may find them driving more slowly in the left lane, driving the wrong way, or pulling out from an intersection, not seeing you. This is another critical observation to look for when analyzing your area. With many parked cars in residentials, it is important to look for people or children; the primary focus here is to scan and maintain a safe speed in these residential areas. Ingrain this with your teen when driving in these residential areas.

- **DangerZones to report**—There is a road near my home which has an intersection, and the curve prior to it is extremely dangerous. The main reason is the traffic on the curve is usually coming at a high rate of speed, and it hard to see if the cars are on the inside lane or the right lane. There are no speed limit signs or warning signs of an upcoming intersection. The drivers coming around the curve are not prepared for someone pulling out from the blinded intersection. The driver pulling out can only see a short distance around the curve also. This is a recipe for a very serious accident! I am working on correcting this situation with the City Traffic Commission. If you have any areas which you feel are unsafe, contact your local city officials and help save someone's life. The life you save may be your own, or your loved ones'. **Update: The City Traffic Commission has put a light now! Yay!**

- **Analyze the weather trends in the area in which you live.** Are there high crosswinds? Is it typically a rainy area? Are there many hydroplaning area possibilities? Is there a lot of fog? Does it snow, and if so, are the roads cleaned in a quick manner? Analyzing and planning for changing weather conditions in your area can prevent you from becoming an offensive driver.

The most important focus concept when it begins to rain is simply reduce your speed according to the changing weather conditions! The rain immediately dissipates the oil on the highway and makes the surface like a wet sheet of glass! The slickest conditions are when it first starts to rain. High winds can create severe crosswinds when driving around hills, mountains, or curves. When working in the transportation business, a large majority of the accidents during inclement weather were usually judged as preventable, with the root cause always being driver's speed too fast for conditions. Use the "Minus 5, Minus 10 MPH" focus concept in inclement weather.

- **Analyze the types of accidents occurring in your area.** When listening to the news or reading an accident news story, I begin to analyze what exactly happened. <u>Almost all the time, you will find the same two root causes were either driver was distracted, or speeding, or both!</u> You will learn by reading the articles, with an aging society, and many in-vehicle distractions you will see the comment "the driver crossed the centerline," causing a head-on collision. In one recent year in the US, there were 260 wrong-way head-on collisions, with 360 people killed! We will cover these accidents and how to prevent them in the Head-on Accidents module. In many of the single-vehicle accidents, when you review them, you will see again the same root causes of speeding: dozing off or distractions! Share all you have learned here with your friends and loved ones.

Remember, here…knowledge is prevention!

Now, spend sufficient quality time with your teen driver, and our goal is to make them DIA-Certified Teen Drivers by executing all the training taught in this curriculum. Important note, during the time you drive each of the first five routes, remember to give a commentary of what you are looking at, what lane strategy you have, and why. Also discuss all the warning signs and analyze all the possible DangerZones you see. Again refer to the 12 DangerZones module. Added routes that your teen drives later should be analyzed together as you continue to follow all your teen's progress.

The First Five Routes Review

➢ Identify the First Five Routes your teen will drive (Home to School, School to Work, Home to Store).

➢ Analyze the 12 DangerZones for each of the First Five Routes.

➢ Determine if there is an alternate and safer route to take for each of the First Five Routes.

➢ Develop and discuss a Strategic Lane Driving Plan for each route.

➢ Parent will drive these routes for the first six months when the teen turns sixteen (before driving) and give Commentary on every route driven.

➢ Teen will start to drive the routes at 16 1/2 or DIA recommendation of age 17. Commentary given on every drive by teen.

➢ Complete DIA DangerZone Roadtest on each observation.

The Twelve DangerZones

After much observation and research, I have determined twelve areas that need to be stressed and understood for improved accident prevention. I have defined these areas as The Twelve DangerZones.

1. Intersections: Controlled and Uncontrolled
2. Inside/Outside Vehicle Distractions
3. Low-Visibility Areas/Curves and Hills
4. Blind-Spot Driving
5. Interstate/Rural Highways
6. Inclement Weather
7. Making Lane Changes
8. Approaching On-Ramps and Off-Ramps
9. Residential Areas
10. Parking Lots
11. Left Turns
12. Night Driving

These 12 DangerZones will be defined and covered in depth in DIA's 12 DangerZones module, copyright 2017, Driving Institute of America.

1. Intersections: Controlled and Uncontrolled

Intersection accidents comprise over 43 percent of all serious accidents (from National Safety Council's Accident Facts). We need to focus on every single intersection by scanning properly and adjusting your speed according to the available visibility.

Even though you have a green light, be prepared for the driver, as we say, who is running late to the airport! At every intersection, GO—PROCEEDING WITH CAUTION! It is very important that you eliminate hasty pullouts at intersections! Also remember, when stopped at intersection preparing to make a left turn, do not turn your wheels until you start to make the turn. Controlled intersections are safer than uncontrolled intersections, so I suggest going to the controlled intersections whenever possible.

2. Inside/Outside Vehicle Distractions

This is the first major root cause of accidents, and the other is speeding. The DIA Pre-drive Check and Setup Routine is the focus concept to eliminate in-vehicle distractions. Review this module completely. Remember, when driving with passengers, avoid looking at them as you are talking when the wheels are rolling! Be organized and keep your vehicle uncluttered!

3. Low-Visibility Areas—Curves and Hills: Very simple focus concept of reducing speed according to available visibility

When you have curves and hills, you cannot see what is around the curve or over the hill. Be a good detector, be prepared for the unexpected and reduce speed accordingly. Of course, with fog you know to reduce speed and if you have fog lights, make sure to use them as needed. When maneuvering on curves, your priority is having proper control of steering with both hands in the event of a blowout.

4. Blind-Spot Driving

Be aware, especially on expressways and interstate highways, when you are in someone else's blind spot! Adjust speed to become staggered and offset as it is defined in the curriculum. You want to ensure they can see you in their mirrors. Minimize the time you are in the other vehicle's blind spot and tap horn if they decide to make lane change. This is why DIA does not like abrupt lane changes by anyone! Also, your proper adjustment of mirrors will help you reduce your blind-spot areas as you drive.

5. Interstate and Rural Highways

When I drive on these highways, my focus is being 100 percent alert, keeping good speed control, and having a safe, strategic lane driving plan. The types of accidents on these highways are usually very serious. Be aware when approaching on-ramps and off-ramps and watch for those not signaling and making abrupt lane changes. Also, if not well-rested, this is not a good recipe for driving on these highways, especially for long trips. Make good decisions!

6. Inclement Weather

We all have seen this scenario: as it is pouring down buckets, someone drives by us as if we were standing still! I call these drivers future statistics! Do not be one of these, as you must reduce speed according to the conditions! I cannot stress this enough, with rain: hydroplaning in rainy weather leads to the lost-control type, or head-on serious accidents. Once you begin to hydroplane, you have no steering control!

When driving on ice and snow, your speed must be even slower and increase the space between the vehicles in front of you. The fifty-car pileups are too many drivers (the groupies) bunched together, driving too fast for conditions. As the weather reporters say, "If you do not have to be on road, stay put!" If this is not possible, then take it slow! Remember the "Minus 5, Minus 10 MPH" focus concept.

7. Changing Lanes

Although this not an area but instead a maneuver; if the focus concept of preplanning a lane change is not executed, the results may not be good. Preplan all your lane changes by checking your mirrors, signaling your intentions ahead of time, quick shoulder check, and gradually sliding into the next lane. If lane change is abrupt, you may risk hitting a car in the other lane trying to pass and not seen in your mirror. I want to know all the lane merges in the areas I drive, so as not to be affected and having to change lanes abruptly. I consider myself a 100-percenter by signaling 100 percent of the time and preplanning every lane change 100 percent of the time also. You want to avoid changing lanes when entering major intersections and especially in the intersection. On my drives, my main objective is to minimize lane changes as much as possible.

8. On-Ramps/Off-Ramps

What I feel is the most important focus concept here is that you start to Detect and Expect possible conflicts when approaching on-ramps (entrances) and off-ramps (exits) on expressways. You must be ready for that driver who realizes they missed the exit and decides to make an abrupt lane change without any signal! I saw one who veered through four lanes traveling approximately 65 miles in about 40–50 yards to make the exit! And yes, I was amazed the vehicle not rolling over. The other major focus concepts are to avoid crossing the solid while line and to blend in accordingly.

9. Residential Areas

These residential areas have lots of low-visibility areas with trees, landscaped hedges, bushes, and parked vehicles on the street, which reduce your visibility. The focus concepts here are proper speed control and scanning for children playing or in front of parked vehicles. Also, when hacking in residential areas, be aware of children and physically check the rear of vehicle prior to backing.

10. Parking Lots

With many vehicles in a very close area, parking lot accidents are the most frequent accidents. The focus concepts are scanning area as you enter and leave the parking lot, scanning for backup lights, people entering with cars preparing to back up. Maintain a safe speed always in the parking lot. Communicate

properly with horn to let people know you are approaching and/or backing up. Stay alert for that anxious driver speeding in the parking lot. When backing up in parking lots, tap your horn and avoid over-backing.

11. Left Turns

Major transportation companies train drivers to avoid making left turns whenever possible. On rural highways (two-lane or four-lane undivided), left turns are very dangerous because of vehicles coming from behind you at a high rate of speed as you are stopped, waiting for oncoming traffic to pass.

On a four-lane undivided highway, my focus concept here is to check my mirrors as I am approaching the intersection where I plan to turn, and signal far enough ahead as I start slowing down so that the vehicle behind me in the same left lane will slow down or try to change into the right lane. I want this driver to go into the right lane. My position is stopped now and watching for oncoming traffic. See module on interstate and rural highways for diagrams. You would do the same if on a two-lane rural highway. Protect your space by controlling the vehicle behind you! Again, remember not to have your wheels turned until you are ready to make the left turn. When having to make left turns, I always try to go to a controlled intersection with traffic lights versus an uncontrolled intersection.

12. Night Driving

With visibility reduced at night, you must "activate your night vision!" You do this by looking for objects that do not give off a reflection. When stopped at a stop sign, preparing to pull out, follow DIA's "In-and-Out Night Vision" focus concept, which is covered in the Night Driving Accidents module.

Speed control is of utmost importance, so my focus concept is "Minus 5, Minus 10 MPH" when driving in unlit areas. Be continually looking for pedestrians as you drive, especially on interstate and express highways, for many times, pedestrians try to cross these highways crossing several lanes. The Government Highway Safety Administration says 1.7 percent of pedestrian fatalities are suicidal. Note: God forbid, but if I were to strike a pedestrian, I would make sure to not leave the scene. The investigation may reflect that the person was going through a divorce or had just lost their job. The person just darted out like a deer, and this is very hard to prevent and was planned by the pedestrian. Communicate with your high beams when needed at night to alert drivers planning to pull out. Remember the lane strategies discussed in the lane strategy module.

The DIA 1520 Rule

Now let's begin with what I strongly believe is the most important focus concept that is crucial to help you survive on our highways. It's very simple, and this is following the 1520 rule. This, to me, is the one habit that will impact the way you drive in a consistent and safe manner. It will eliminate you from speeding, tailgating, abrupt lane changes, making hasty pullouts at all types of intersections (controlled or uncontrolled), and simply not being offensive behind the wheel!

If I were conducting a three-hour seminar and at the start of seminar we were told, "There's a tornado approaching in our direction, and we will have to end the seminar," but we had 2–3 minutes to cover anything we wanted to share, I would discuss the 1520 rule—IT IS THAT IMPORTANT!

You must understand this rule needs to be the strongest disciplined habit in your driving routine. How the 1520 rule works is very simple; you want to depart at a time that will get you to arrive at your destination 15 to 20 minutes minimum prior to scheduled time. An example is, if you are scheduled to be at a location at 0800 hours, you would depart with the plan of arriving at 0740–0745. Again, you will find your drive becoming less stressful, and you will be not hurried, more observant, and aware of other drivers. It will help you become a better detector, allow you time to compensate for others, and prepare you for other drivers' offensive habits.

I wrote a newspaper article regarding my training, and one of the readers, who happened to be in his seventies called me and said, "This 1520 rule really makes a lot of sense and I will plan to use this focus concept when I drive." A fellow driver working with me in the transportation business for over twenty-seven years, to my surprise, said the very same thing after hearing about my "1520 rule" focus concept. This habit by itself is HUGE! If everyone lived by the 1520 rule, driving on our highways would be so much safer for us all! I cannot stress this enough: living by the 1520 Rule will change the way you drive and can save your life. Remember, 15-20 minutes is the minimum time you should plan ahead. If weather conditions, or traffic is bad, you want to leave earlier.

DIA #1 FOCUS CONCEPT: BE A DISCIPLINED DIA 1520 DRIVER!

#1 Focus Concept: The DIA 1520 Rule

You must be disciplined, by planning to arrive at your destination a minimum of 15 to 20 minutes ahead of schedule on every driving mission.

This is the #1 focus concept and the key to eliminate speeding, aggressive driving, and all serious types of accidents.

BE A DISCIPLINED 1520 DRIVER!

Why Be a DIA 1520 Driver?

It eliminates

1. Speeding
2. Tailgating
3. **Hasty** pullouts at intersections
4. Abrupt lane changes
5. Being a "**Groupie**"
6. Running Red Lights
7. Lost-control accidents
8. Rollover accidents

It compensates for other drivers' actions or inactions.

Also, it makes you more of an In-control driver vs. an Offensive driver.

DIA Pre-Drive Vehicle Inspection

When I first started working in the transportation field, I remember seeing a sign that read, "YOU ARE ABOUT TO ENTER THE MOST DANGEROUS PLACE IN THE WORLD—THE PUBLIC HIGHWAYS! DRIVE SAFELY!"

Also, as a professional driver, taking care of my vehicle was extremely important. As professional drivers, prior to driving our vehicle, each driver performs a complete PRE-DRIVE INSPECTION and a complete POST-DRIVE INSPECTION at the end of the day. It is critical for you to know the condition of your vehicle and conduct periodic inspections of your vehicle. Although you do not have to do it as often as those who drive daily as a profession, you need to check these items periodically.

The condition of the tires is crucial; checking for proper inflation, damaged tread, or low tread should be a routine. Signal lights are also vital to communicate with other traffic. The backup lights/brake lights are always items that I check more frequently. My thoughts are, if I were to put my vehicle in reverse and the backup lights are not working, I am looking at a possible accident! Your backup lights communicate to others! Your brakes should be tested every time simply by putting the vehicle in gear, then depressing the brakes to ensure they are working properly. Check these with a family member or friend occasionally.

Also become completely familiar with all the instrumentation in your vehicle. This is covered in the module DIA's 16-Year-Old's Driving Plan.

Inoperable Mirrors = An Accident Waiting to Happen!

DIA Pre-Drive Check and Setup Routine

The next important step is the <u>DIA Pre-Drive Check and Setup Routine</u> to help eliminate all in-vehicle distractions! This is especially imperative with teen drivers. You need to preselect your radio station (have all your favorite stations preset ahead of time). If playing a CD/ IPOD/MP3 player, get this setup prior to putting your vehicle in motion. <u>Set up all your gadgets before departure. Also maintain the inside of the vehicle area clutter-free, with all articles secured properly! Be organized!</u>

And most important, ELIMINATE TEXTING! Again, make this a disciplined routine. Phone calls and texting need to be done at a safe place off the road. I want to scream "GET OFF THE PHONE AND DRIVE!" when I see drivers texting while the wheels are rolling! It is easy to spot someone ahead of you texting because of their frequent weaving in and out of their lane. <u>I make it a point to avoid passing and getting in front of them until they turn off.</u>

Next, adjust your mirrors properly. Focus on not overlapping your rearview mirrors, which increases your blind spots. This is covered in the next module (The Importance of Proper Mirror Adjustment).

<u>The Pre-Drive Check and Setup Routine is the solution for eliminating in-vehicle distractions, and it helps keep your eyes focused on the road instead.</u>

The DIA FOCUS CONCEPT here is "WHEN THE WHEELS ARE ROLLING, YOU CAN'T BE LOOKING DOWN, TEXTING, OR LOOKING AT ANY PASSENGERS!" YOUR FOCUS IS 100 PERCENT ON THE ROAD!

Also test horn by tapping to ensure proper communication.

DIA FOCUS CONCEPT: The HORN IS FREE TO USE. NOT USING IT CAN BE EXPENSIVE! We will cover this in the Proper Horn Usage module.

ALERT: When you drop an article while the vehicle is in motion, the tendency is to bend down to pick it up. You will most likely turn the steering wheel toward the side you are bending, and this can easily result in striking a fixed object or losing control! This type of accident occurs frequently. Remember, stay organized!

DIA® Pre-Drive Check and Setup Routine

1. **Your vehicle in proper working condition**: lights, signals, horn, brakes, tires, and mirrors
2. **Become familiarized completely with vehicle instrumentation** before driving **(especially for teens!)**
3. **Secure all articles (purse, bottles, miscellaneous items) and pets! No flip-flops! STAY ORGANIZED! (*Dropping articles)**
4. **Preset radio, iPod, MP3 player before vehicle moves!**
5. **Fan mirrors out to minimize blind spots to obtain maximum rear visibility.**

This routine is the solution for eliminating distractions and preventing an accident.

The Importance of Proper Mirror Adjustment

What is covered in this module is understanding the importance of <u>proper mirror adjustment for maximizing visibility to the rear.</u> You will see the correct and incorrect mirror adjustments in the diagrams below. Your mirrors are vital in helping you avoid being struck from behind, in performing safe lane changes, and when having to back up.

ALERT: If you are driving a vehicle without any one of your mirrors, you need to replace the missing mirror immediately! You are asking for an accident!

The diagram on the left is an example of incorrect mirror adjustment. These mirrors are too far in; they overlap and minimize your overall visibility to the rear of your vehicle.

Note: If you sit straight and turn your head to the left mirror and see too much of your vehicle, or your face, you need to pull mirror out to barely see the side of your vehicle. Do this also for the right mirror. Fanning mirrors out will maximize your vision to the rear and minimize your blind spot on both sides!

The diagram on the right is the correct mirror adjustment. The mirrors adjusted correctly will give you maximum vision to the rear. Again, this adjustment is critically important for safe lane changes. The middle mirror is the key when having these mirrors adjusted this way. <u>You must use all three mirrors together as you drive.</u> When I drive, this is an immediate check, especially if someone else has driven my vehicle.

The Importance of Proper Mirror Adjustment

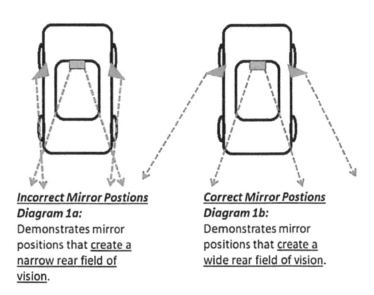

Incorrect Mirror Postions
Diagram 1a:
Demonstrates mirror
positions that <u>create a
narrow rear field of
vision</u>.

Correct Mirror Postions
Diagram 1b:
Demonstrates mirror
positions that <u>create a
wide rear field of vision</u>.

➢ <u>Focus Concept:</u>

Maximize your rear field of vision and minimize your blind spot with proper mirror adjustments and using <u>all three mirrors together</u>.

The Four Types of Drivers

The four types of drivers are (1) The Complacent/Aggressive driver, (2) The Paranoid/Slow driver, (3) The Elderly driver, and (4) the DIA 100 percent In-Control driver. OUR MISSION IS TO MAKE YOU THE DIA 100 PERCENT IN-CONTROL DRIVER.

1. The Complacent/Aggressive Driver

The complacent/aggressive driver is not a disciplined driver. This driver regularly departs late to work, church, or whatever destination they are going to on a consistent basis. This hastiness makes this driver aggressive, offensive, and careless. The most common behaviors are changing lanes without signaling, making abrupt lane changes, easily being distracted, running red lights, rolling through stop signs, making hasty pullouts at intersections, driving too fast in parking lots, tailgating, missing exits, cutting people off at on-ramps/off-ramps, and of course, speeding consistently (even during inclement weather).

Usually this driver has other in-vehicle distractions such as texting, or eating on the run. When I see this driver, I just think, "Another statistic, sooner or later," and get out of their way!

The teen driver falls into this category also because of being hyper and easily distracted. The teen driver makes rash decisions like hastily pulling out at intersections and is very inexperienced in visual detecting habits!

Again, please understand this: by being aggressive and offensive, you become less defensive! This means you have less time to react to the possible conflicts and dangers of the road. Aggressive drivers wear out their brakes and tires sooner, blast their horn more, skid more, and waste more gas!

If this sounds like you, your family and I congratulate you for getting this book! Yay! HASTINESS = OFFENSIVE/AGGRESSIVE DRIVER = FUTURE STATISTIC!

The Four Types of Drivers

1. The Complacent/Aggressive Driver

- is not a disciplined driver!
- is usually running late!
- does not signal!
- weaves in and out
- makes hasty pullouts
- tailgates
- is on the phone, or texting
- **IS A FUTURE STATISTIC! IS THIS YOU?**

Example:

Cartoon drawn by Steve Kelley

2. The Paranoid/Slow Driver

The Paranoid/Slow driver usually drives slower, may have been in previous accidents, and therefore is more hesitant and indecisive. The paranoid driver who has been in an accident usually overfocuses on one area instead of looking all around. If they previously were involved in an intersection accident where they were struck on the passenger side, they have the tendency to focus more on their right side and not check to the left side.

Also, they could be new to the area and unfamiliar with the street system. Out-of-state license plates are a tip-off of these drivers. These unfamiliar drivers are erratic and make abrupt lane changes without signaling. Teen drivers also fall into this area due to inexperience and unawareness of the area and lane endings at major intersections.

At all on-ramps or exit ramps, you need to be a good detector for these drivers, and blend in when these drivers immediately decide to cut you off, taking the exit unexpectedly in front of you! On-ramps and Off-ramps are one of the 12 DangerZones, and you must be prepared for unexpected lane changes from these drivers. When you see the next exit sign 100–200 feet ahead, this becomes your detect-and-expect moment of any possible conflicts, and be prepared for someone to cut you off!

Again, the focus concept is to blend in and back off if necessary to avoid being sideswiped. This is called being STAGGERED; remember this word, for it is lifesaver when you perform this out on the road daily. Staggered means being offset and having an opening into at least one lane whenever possible, and especially to the right lane if you are driving in the left lane.

The Four Types of Drivers

2. The Paranoid/Slow Driver

- ➤ has been in a <u>previous accident</u>
- ➤ has tunnel vision at times
- ➤ is unfamiliar with the area
  (*Look for OUT-OF-STATE LICENSE PLATES)
- ➤ is a new teen driver

3. The Elderly Driver

- ➤ has poor hearing
- ➤ has poor vision
- ➤ has poor health
- ➤ has poor reflexes

3. The Elderly Driver

Society is getting older! With over 74 million baby boomers on our roads today, the head-on collision where the elderly driver crossed the centerline has become more prevalent. I believe accidents involving our elderly drivers will continue to get worse!

The other typical accident is where the elderly driver hit the gas instead of the brake and plowed into a building or struck many pedestrians on the street. We must be aware of these drivers when we are out on the highways. They are easy to spot, as they tend to drive very slowly in the right lane, although sometimes they may be in the left lane. Their vision is impaired once in they are in late seventies or early eighties; therefore, you want to ensure to be prepared and expect that they do not see you!

Very important: any elderly drivers in your family need to be evaluated periodically for their driving skills. An assessment needs to be made if they are still qualified to be safe drivers on the highways. Also, complete the DIA DangerZone Roadtests and develop a Strategic Lane Driving Plan for each driving route if they will continue to drive. I suggest minimizing the number of driving routes they have (i.e., to grocery store, church, pharmacy). We made the decision to take my mother off the road and most likely prevented a possible accident.

This is a decision every family with very elderly drivers needs to review and take whatever steps needed to prevent a serious accident with your loved one.

4. The DIA 100 Percent In-Control Driver

This is your ultimate goal! To develop new DIA disciplined driving habits, and they become 100 percent consistent each time you drive! The DIA In-control driver is never complacent, thinking, "I am a great driver" and understands being focused on the driving mission 100 percent until reaching the final destination. Like we say, drive like a surgeon. A surgeon is 100 percent focused, not 99.8 percent, but 100 percent on the operation of the patient until the surgery is completed. The surgeon is not distracted or in a hurry, and this is how you should drive also. Again, the most important first step of the DIA in-control type of driver is being disciplined in the 1520 rule. This will immediately improve your driving mindset and reduce any major driving concerns. I am being repetitive regarding The 1520 Rule, but this is for retention purposes.

The DIA In-Control type of driver is continually learning to become a better detector of any accident possibilities and to be proactive instead of reactive. Remember being reactive is usually too late. When you read about someone who was killed in a head-on collision due to an oncoming car crossing the centerline, this means the other person was not detecting and expecting and did not have an opening into the right lane to move over. This driver was not prepared in advance to immediately change lanes when the vehicle started crossing the centerline! You need to be prepared for the distracted driver who crosses the centerline!

When you make the decision of going into the left lane, you will understand this, and you will know that your lane strategy is to be staggered/offset when possible. We will cover this in the module "The Head-on Accidents."

The Four Types of Drivers

4. The DIA IN-CONTROL

Driver

- ➢ is 100 percent focused and In Control from Point A to Point B
- ➢ follows the 19 DIA Good Driver elements
- ➢ is YOUR ULTIMATE GOAL!

Learn to "Drive Like a Surgeon"

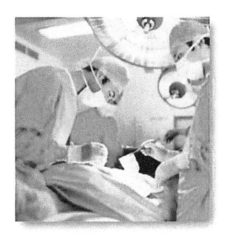

- A surgeon is **100 percent focused** on the patient **until the surgery is completed.**
- **A DIA-Certified Good Driver must also be 100 percent focused and In Control on their driving from Point A to Point B.**

Detect and Expect

- Like **The Lion in the Jungle** is observant by scanning for the hunter who may kill him! He **detects and expects** for his survival!

- You too must learn the importance of **detecting and expecting** on the roadways to avoid possible conflicts ahead of time.

Analyze Your Area

Now, I want you to think about the area where you live, and let's analyze it. Do you live in an area which has lots of curves and hills? If so, you have many low-visibility areas. These are what I call possible DangerZones and should be approached at slower speeds due to reduced visibility. You do not know what is on the other side of hill, or around the curve. Even more caution is required when the roads are wet from rain or snow. You want to know what roads become hydroplaning possibilities and reduce your speed in these areas accordingly.

Do you live in an area where deer and other wildlife are plentiful? This creates a huge problem, especially at night. As mentioned earlier, activating your night vision and reducing your speed (Minus 5, Minus 10 MPH) will help you in these areas. I purchased the deer whistles that are supposed to keep the deer away. You can purchase these whistles at your local auto parts store.

Other areas to analyze: are there older residents driving regularly in your neighborhood (i.e. retirement communities, senior citizen activity center)? This adds many drivers in your area who drive slower, do not have the best hearing, vision, or reflexes. You need to be aware and compensate for them, and not drop your guard with these elderly drivers.

Does the area where you live have tourist attractions? This means many drivers who are unaware of where they are going, which means abrupt lane changes, slower driving, and unawareness of exit ramps or lane endings.

Have you noticed families with toddlers on your block? This is an area you need to be very focused on, especially when backing out of your driveway. Make it a habit to physically check the rear of your vehicle prior to backing! When you read the paper or listen to the news, analyze what were the root causes of these accidents that occurred in your area.

Do you have many pedestrians and bicyclists in the areas you drive? If so, are they out riding their bicycles at night? In my city, there are many bicyclists and pedestrians in the downtown area at night; therefore, my night vision is focused and activated looking out for them.

There are several areas where I live that are very prone to having head-on accidents. I have become very aware of these roads and plan my lane strategies accordingly when driving these roads (undivided highways with curves or hills, and frontage roads).

One more area to review in your area would be the local bars and nightspots which may result in many DUI drivers on your daily routes.

So, analyze your area well and keep abreast of the news involving anything dealing with driving and vehicle accidents in your area.

DIA Safety Tips—<u>Analyze Your Area!</u>

Are there

- Lots of seniors or toddlers living in your area?
- Lots of wildlife, especially deer? Heavy tree-lined areas?
- High-frequency accident areas?
- Hills and curves?
- Low-visibility areas?
- Flood/high-water areas?

Pay attention to news/radio reports and analyze the accidents that you hear about.

Strategic Lane Driving Plan

This module is so critically important! We will review lane strategies, lane situations, and lane endings. Many drivers, if asked, "Are you a left lane driver?" would likely respond by saying, "I'm not sure." Driving approximately 1,000 miles a week for over eleven years, I encountered many driving situations. I learned that you must have a strategic lane driving plan even on your way to and from work, and on your regular errand driving missions also.

Scenario: On a four-lane undivided highway, when I need to pass a slow-moving vehicle that is in the right lane and I make the decision to go into the left lane, I ensure that I am not being a blind-spot driver, and drive where the driver in the right lane can see me in their mirror.

Most importantly, my goal is to he staggered/offset and not pass this vehicle until the oncoming traffic has passed. <u>By passing the vehicle in the right lane when oncoming traffic is approaching, I may become immediately boxed in! Should the oncoming vehicle cross the centerline or if the vehicle in right lane changes into the left lane, I would most likely be in an instant head-on collision!</u> If I wait until there is no oncoming traffic and the vehicle in the right lane changes into left lane, I could still avoid being a possible serious accident. Anytime I can avoid being boxed in the left lane, this becomes my strategic driving plan. This is how I try to drive in this situation. Again, <u>I drive most of my routes with the intention of minimizing lane changes as much as possible.</u> This should be your goal also.

Here is a lane strategy for going over a bridge/overpass (at night) or curve on a four-lane <u>divided</u> highway. I will never go over the crest of the bridge/overpass, or a sharp curve in the left lane on a four-lane <u>divided</u> highway (especially at night). Here's why. The reason is you may have another car whose driver thinks the road is only two lanes (due to being unfamiliar with the area, or under the influence), and ends up going in the wrong direction!

This accident occurs more at night and early morning hours (especially high on Friday through Sunday morning window). **This is the wrong-way head-on collision** you hear about on the news, where one driver was going in the wrong direction. If there are three lanes (on a six-lane <u>divided</u> highway), I myself prefer to drive in the middle lane. People can get killed instantly in this type of freak accident!

In one year recently, there were 260 wrong-way driver head-on accidents in the United States! 'These head-on accidents resulted in 360 fatalities. These people are no longer here! Again, you should always have a strategic lane driving plan.

One weekend, there were <u>two wrong-way head-on accidents, resulting in eleven fatalities</u>! One driver was driving the wrong way intentionally (suicidal) at 110 miles per hour! We will cover this more in the Head-on Accidents module.

Have a Strategic Lane Driving Plan

Especially on your regular routes, such as to work/store/church

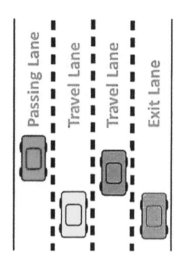

- **Know your LANE MERGES!**
- **Preplan** your lane changes.
- **Avoid abrupt** lane changes.
- **Minimize** lane changes.

➢ **Focus Concepts:** Detect and Expect and **BLEND IN.**

PROACTIVE vs. REACTIVE

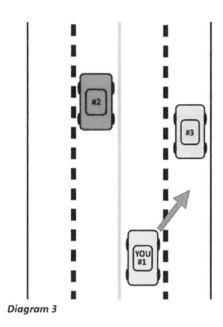

Diagram 3

➢ <u>**SCENARIO**</u>**: You are in the left lane and wanting to pass Vehicle #3 on your right. You notice Vehicle #2 drifting toward the centerline.**

➢ If you are in the left lane, make sure you have an opening to your right lane in case the oncoming car drifts across the centerline.

➢ <u>**FOCUS CONCEPT**</u>: When making the decision to be in the left lane, <u>be proactive versus reactive</u> in this situation. BEING REACTIVE IS TOO LATE!

Avoid getting "boxed in" when driving in the left lane whenever possible. Try to be staggered and proactive, with an opening into the right lane.

STAGGERED—A Very Important Word

Being staggered means when driving on a divided or undivided four-lane or six-lane road, <u>you are offset from other vehicles.</u> <u>By being staggered in the middle lane, you have an opening to the right, or left lane, and offset from the vehicles on either side. If you are not staggered, you are either boxed in or in someone's blind spot. As DIA states, minimize the time you are in someone else's blind spot.</u> Being staggered gives you an opening to avoid conflicts. *<u>Also, when you are staggered, you want to be where the drivers in other vehicles ahead can see you in their side mirrors. This is a very important focus concept.</u>

*When you have two left turning lanes, you want to immediately get staggered/offset to avoid a possible sideswipe situation. See Diagrams.

Staggered—Don't Be a Blind-Spot Driver!

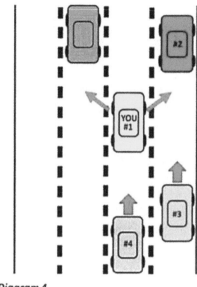

Diagram 4

- ➤ **SCENARIO:** **Vehicles #3 and #4 are driving the same speed, causing Vehicle #4 to be consistently in Vehicle #3's blind spot. You are <u>staggered</u> between all vehicles. <u>Staggered</u> means offset, having an opening to either the right or left lane.**
  - ✓ **If you need to pass a vehicle, remain <u>staggered</u> as much as possible by adjusting your speed before passing the other vehicle and minimize your time in the other vehicle's blind spot.**
  - ✓ **If there are multiple lanes, remain <u>staggered</u> in the middle lane** so you always have an opening on both sides if you need to avoid a collision.

- ➤ **FOCUS CONCEPT:** Eliminate blind-spot driving by being <u>staggered</u> as much as possible.

Which Is the Safest Lane?

Which is the safest lane? This knowledge will give you the understanding that ultimately, whatever lane you decide to be in, you must make it the safest lane according to each situation. I always have a rationale and plan for being in a certain lane. This is how I try to drive.

FOUR LANES DIVIDED and UNDIVIDED

As mentioned in the module Strategic Lane Driving Plan, when I make the decision of being in the left lane, (1) I understand the importance of always trying to have an opening to change to the right lane as much as possible, (2) I am prepared for oncoming traffic to veer over the centerline, (3) I try not to pass a vehicle in the right lane until oncoming traffic has cleared and avoid getting boxed in whenever possible, and (4) when in the left lane, I am traveling at the posted speed limit. You do not want to be in the left lane going 5–10 miles slower than the posted speed limit.

When I make the decision of being in the right lane, I am aware of bicyclists, pedestrians, lane merges, vehicles turning, or pulling out, and animals (i.e. deer, livestock in rural areas). This is crucial, especially driving at night (activate your night vision). If the road does not have a shoulder area, be aware of low-visibility areas such as trees. Also very important when approaching a hill or curve in the right lane: this minimizes your visibility; therefore, simply reduce your speed, and be prepared for any possible conflicts over the hill or around the curve. Being in the right lane will have more stopping and accelerating also. Again, when there are three or four lanes, I choose the two inside left lanes (eight-lane expressways divided) until reaching my planned exit off-ramp.

SIX LANES DIVIDED

If I have three lanes, the one lane I take is usually the middle lane and attempt to be staggered as much as possible. If I am in the left lane, I want to follow the same focus concept discussed when being in the middle lane, which is to always have an opening to the middle lane whenever possible. When I am in the right lane, I am prepared for merging traffic and lane reductions. I usually go into the middle or far-left lanes to avoid these types of changes. Once I get close to my exit, then I preplan my lane change and merge safely into the right lane. See Diagram.

TWO-LANE RURAL AND CITY

Very important on the two-lane rural roads is to stay in your lane, especially when rounding sharp curves. The tendency is to make the turn too wide or too sharp crossing your designated lane. DIA focus concept is to tap your horn prior to negotiating any sharp curve. This will alert oncoming traffic that could be making a turn too sharp, which is a tendency especially on rural roads. Be prepared for oncoming traffic and those attempting to pass the other oncoming traffic.

Which Is the Safest Lane?

Lane	Possible Consequence
Left Lane =	More possible head-on/ *Be staggered whenever possible and proactive
Middle Lane =	Staggered, not in blind spot, is a better option
Right Lane =	Watch for pedestrians or animals (day or night)

(At Night)
Minus 5 Minus 10

Know Your Lane Endings!

Knowing your lane endings plays a huge part in making your drive smooth, less stressful, and safe. That is why I put an exclamation mark on this module title. Some drivers are aware of all their lane endings to the grocery store, the cleaners, but when it comes to other major intersections, they lack this knowledge.

Learn and observe the signs that designate what each lane will do as soon as possible, at all intersections, but especially at all major intersections. <u>Again, these major intersections become "detect and expect" zones along with on-ramps and off-ramps.</u> Start detecting for other drivers possibly making abrupt lane changes and possibly cutting you off!

Focus on blending in, in these on-ramp/off-ramp areas. Also, <u>do not cross the solid white line when entering or exiting ramps</u>! Test your family members also so they also become knowledgeable in all their lane endings.

Preplan all lane changes should you be in the wrong lane of where you want to go. It is better to proceed to the next intersection than to make an abrupt, unsafe lane change!

Know All Your Lane Endings

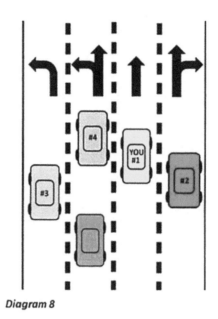

Diagram 8

> **SCENARIO**: you are approaching a multiple-lane intersection
>   ✓ Look and <u>know all lane ending signs</u> and markings on the roads you travel frequently.
>   ✓ It is imperative that you know all your lane endings when approaching any intersection, <u>to avoid abrupt lane changes</u> on your part, <u>and be a good detector for abrupt lane changes by other drivers as well.</u>

> **FOCUS CONCEPT**: KNOW ALL YOUR LANE ENDINGS AHEAD OF TIME of all your regular driving routes.

Preventing the Seven Most Serious Accidents

1. **Intersection Accidents**
2. **Lost-Control/Rollover Accidents**
3. **Head-on Accidents**
4. **Striking Fixed Objects**
5. **Pedestrian, Bicycle, and Motorcycle Accidents**
6. **Night Driving Accidents**
7. **Freak Accidents**

Preventing Accident #1: Intersection Accidents

- Intersection accidents are the cause for over 43 percent of all fatal accidents (National Safety Council)

- Let us look at the **root causes** and solutions for several types of intersection accidents.

PREVENTING INTERSECTION ACCIDENTS

Intersection accidents account for over 43 percent of vehicle fatalities according to the National Safety Council. This module will cover several types of intersection accidents and describe all the focus concepts to help you prevent being in these different types of intersection accidents. The majority of intersection accidents are caused just by being in a hurry! Simple as that! In these accident diagrams, we will make you VEHICLE #1. We use VEHICLE #2 as the other driver.

The "But I Had the Green Light!" Intersection Accident

This is the #1 intersection accident type occurring each and every day. Thousands of drivers have been killed or seriously injured when they in fact had the green light! Let us review this in detail. You are Vehicle #1 approaching the intersection with a red light; it then turns to green. You continue to enter the intersection and then CRASH!

Vehicle #2 ran the red light! What happened? Upon seeing the green light, your brain processed it as go. You thought that all the cross traffic had stopped, but Vehicle #2 (running late to destination) continued without ever intending to stop, because of running late to their destination (i.e. airport, work, or meeting), and crashed into your vehicle! Also, the building on the right blocked your vision; therefore, you should have slowed down to obtain sufficient visibility and clearance before entering this intersection.

The DIA focus concept here is "A green light will mean go only if all cross traffic is stopping! It means GO—PROCEEDING WITH CAUTION!"

Always avoid changing lanes near the entrance of the intersection or in the intersection! Remember, at all uncontrolled intersections without any stop signs, yield to the vehicle on the right!

"But I Had the Green Light!" Intersection Accident

➢ **SCENARIO**: Traffic light is green; your visibility is blocked by a building or tree. The other car's driver is distracted looking at Christmas lights and runs the red light.

➢ **FOCUS CONCEPT**: Reduce your speed when approaching a blind intersection until you are sure it is clear of cross traffic. CLEAR ALL INTERSECTIONS BEFORE ENTERING!

➢ **EXAMPLE**: For someone running late to the airport, the light could be PURPLE—the driver will run it anyway!

The "Parking Lot or Stop Sign Intersection" Pullout Accident

Scenario #1: You are Vehicle #1 driving in the right lane as you are approaching a parking lot entrance/exit to a retail store. You notice Vehicle #2 approximately 200–300 feet ahead; you have "detected the vehicle, and now you must expect" what Vehicle #2 will do. Remember, this driver may he impaired, in a hurry, or not see you at all!

Your focus concept is to be prepared in the event that Vehicle #2's wheels start moving. You cannot, and must not, think Vehicle #2's driver has seen you (especially if you are on a motorcycle or bicycle), and understand they could be distracted or running behind, so they may make a hasty pullout!

There was a study which explained that we have a natural blind spot when we look sometimes to the left or right. This explains why sometimes we have looked to the left and did not see a vehicle, then the second time we looked left, there was a vehicle! We say to ourselves, "Where did that car come from!?" So be prepared.

By detecting and expecting, you become a proactive driver instead of the reactive driver who may end up in an accident. The focus concept is to tap your horn as soon as you see Vehicle #2's wheels beginning to roll! This will help driver in Vehicle #2 make a decision to stay. Not tapping leads to the possibility of blasting horn because Vehicle #2 pulls out quickly and you realize you may be in trouble! Remember, tapping your horn is proactive—blasting your horn is reactive! Detect and expect!

Scenario #2: Now, let's say you are the vehicle at the exit of the parking lot, and you are preparing to exit onto the main highway. YOUR DIA FOCUS CONCEPT is not to be hasty but TAKE AN EXTRA SECOND to judge the speed of cross traffic. Don't make a rash decision and pull out! When you notice the vehicle driving at an excessive speed, you then make the decision to wait. Remember, you are following the 1520 rule, so you are not in a hurried state!

The "Hasty Pullout" Intersection Accident

This situation is similar to parking lot exit/entrance intersection. Vehicle #2 is running behind and in a big hurry. At the stop sign, the driver makes the hasty pullout! You have detected ahead of time, and you are proactive by slowing down, avoiding a possible intersection accident.

When you are finding yourself in a hurry, eliminate from becoming hasty at any intersection. **The hasty pullout, again, is the reason for so many accidents!** Be proactive by being patient! If you are a motorcyclist or bicyclist in this scenario, use extra caution, for it is harder for Vehicle #2, who is pulling out to see you. I witnessed a motorcyclist strike a vehicle pulling out because the vehicle pulling out hastily did not see motorcyclist.

NOTE: If you are consistently rolling through stop signs, sooner or later, your chances of being in an accident will catch up with you.

When you are the planning to pull out again, take the extra second to judge the speed of the cross traffic and perform the DIA (five-point) left-right-left-right-left scan. If you have large side mirrors, a vehicle can be hidden behind the mirror, so you can do "the rocking chair" and ensure cross traffic is clear. Avoid these hasty and rash decisions when pulling out altogether.

Intersection Hasty Pullouts by You

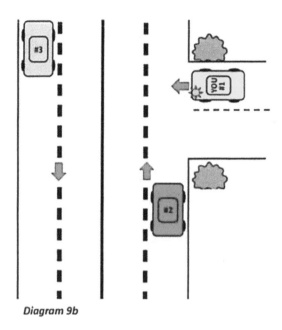

Diagram 9b

➢ <u>Scenario</u>: **You are Vehicle #1 waiting to pull out into traffic.**
- ✓ Sometimes vehicles are driving at an unexpected high rate of speed, and this is a recipe for an accident if you do not take an **extra second or two to judge the speed of cross traffic in all directions.**

➢ <u>**Focus concept: AVOID HASTY pullouts by looking and judging cross-traffic speed.**</u>

*We all have a natural blind spot that occurs occasionally.**

Intersection Hasty Pullouts by Others

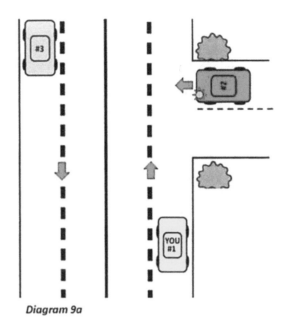

Diagram 9a

> <u>Scenario</u>: **You are in the right lane and detect that Vehicle #2 is ready to pull out.**
>   ✓ **Detect and expect** means to be alert and aware of a collision possibility.
>   ✓ Immediately as you see Vehicle #2's wheels start moving, be **proactive**, tap horn to let Vehicle #2 see you are approaching. This **alerts Vehicle #2 to make the decision to wait. But be prepared!**
>   ✓ <u>**Focus Concept**</u>: **Detect and expect for HASTY pullout drivers.**

The "Overly Courteous Drivers" Intersection Accident

Believe it or not, there are times when drivers can be overly courteous. You may have experienced this situation when you were in heavy traffic and you were trying to cross the highway. The vehicle in the left lane creates an opening for you to cross the lane, the driver in the next lane (middle lane), also leaves an open space. Now they have created a huge blind spot!

There is an approaching car in the far-right lane whose driver does not see your vehicle crossing and crashes into you! What I do is wave them on and wait until I can cross safely.

The diagram below will show you the correct steps to take regarding this situation. The focus concept is, when a driver tries to create the opening for you, just wait until all traffic lanes are clear.

The "Overly Courteous Drivers" Intersection Accident (1)

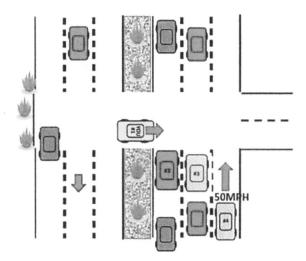

➤ <u>Scenario</u>: **This is an uncontrolled intersection. You are in Vehicle #1 attempting to cross the intersection. Vehicles #2 and #3 stop to be courteous, which creates a blind spot. You do not see Vehicle #4 coming at a high rate of speed.**

The "Overly Courteous Drivers" Intersection Accident (2)

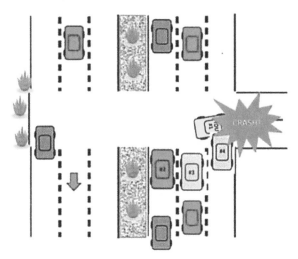

➤ <u>Scenario</u>: **This is an uncontrolled intersection. You are in Vehicle #1 attempting to cross the intersection. Vehicles #2 and #3 stop to be courteous, which creates a blind spot. You do not see Vehicle #4 coming at a high speed.**

➤ <u>Focus Concept</u>: **When drivers try to be courteous in this manner, <u>wave them on</u> and <u>wait until all the lanes are clear</u> before proceeding.**

The "Hidden Vehicle" Intersection Accident

In this scenario, you are preparing to make a left turn onto a four-lane undivided highway, and you plan on going into the inside left lane. You notice a vehicle coming from the left side (in the right lane), with his right signal light on, slows down and starts to turn. You decide to make the left turn. What you did not see was the vehicle hidden behind this vehicle in the inside left lane, going 60 mph! CRASH!

If you pull out making the left turn, you must also make sure the inside lane is clear and not blocked by the vehicle in the right lane! Again, being in a hurry and hasty will result in a very serious accident in this situation.

DIA Focus Concept: Avoid being hasty—be patient, wait, and check for the possible hidden vehicle in the inside left lane! See diagram.

The "Hidden Vehicle" Intersection Accident (1)

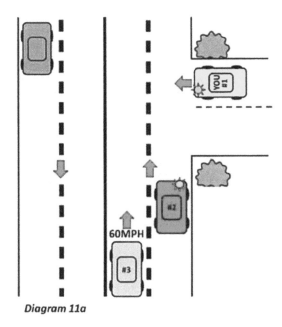

Diagram 11a

> ➤ <u>**Scenario:**</u> **You are Vehicle #1 waiting to pull out into traffic and you see Vehicle #2 slowing down, with its right blinker on, planning to turn. Vehicle #3 is hidden from your view.**
>   ✓ Before you pull out <u>knowing that Vehicle #2 is turning right and slows down,</u> **<u>wait to see if there is a hidden vehicle</u>** on the inside left lane that could be going straight at a high speed. Do not pull out until you clear the other lane!

The "Hidden Vehicle" Intersection Accident (2)

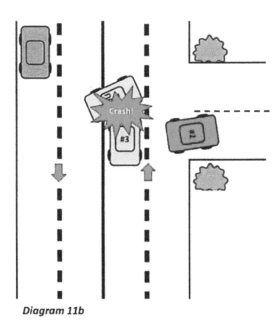

Diagram 11b

➤ <u>Scenario:</u> **You are Vehicle #1 waiting to pull out into traffic and you see Vehicle #2 slowing down, with right blinker on. Vehicle #3 is hidden from your view.**
   ✓ Before you pull out knowing <u>that Vehicle #2 is going to turn right</u>, **wait** to see if there is a **hidden vehicle** on the inside left lane that could be going straight at a high speed!
➤ <u>Focus Concept</u>: **Be aware of hidden vehicles in other lanes and <u>wait until both lanes are clear</u> before pulling out.**

The "Lights Are On, But No One's Home!" Intersection Accident

I call this one the "lights are on, but no one's home" intersection accident. You are at a stop sign, preparing to pull out to a major street. You look to your left, and Vehicle #2 has their right-turn signal on but does not know it is on! You pull out, and CRASH! Vehicle #2 strikes you, going 60 miles per hour!

As a DIA-Certified Good Driver, you understand not to rely on this vehicle turning UNTIL you see vehicle beginning to slow down. <u>Hesitation, and not hastiness, is the focus concept here.</u>

There have been many intersection accidents caused by the driver not knowing his or her right-turn signal was on. We have all done this ourselves on occasion.

DIA Focus Concept: Again, don't get hasty and pull out <u>until you see the vehicle beginning to slow down</u>!

The "Lights Are On, But No One's Home" Intersection Accident

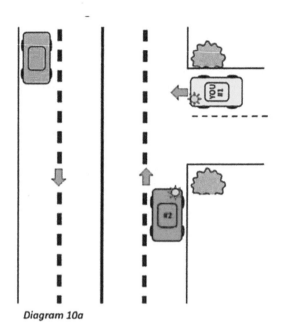

Diagram 10a

> ➤ **Scenario:** You are Vehicle #1 waiting to pull out into traffic, and you see Vehicle #2 with its right blinker on.
> > ✓ Sometimes vehicles have blinker flashing, but **they are not aware that it is on!** If you hastily decide to pull out, thinking Vehicle #2 is going to turn, you are in for a high-speed crash!

The "Lights Are On, But No One's Home" Intersection Accident (2)

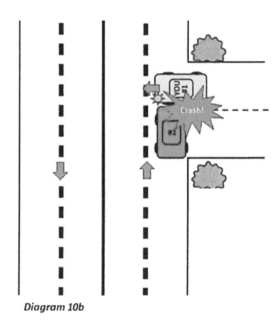

Diagram 10b

> ➤ **Focus Concept:** <u>Do not get HASTY</u> and pull out until you are 100 percent sure the vehicle is going to turn, begins to slow down, and the other lane is clear!

The "Lane Change" Intersection Accident

Here, you are preparing to pull out and make a left turn onto a four-lane undivided road. The left side is clear, you look to the right, and there are three cars in the far-right lane. You plan on going into the inside lane. At the same moment that you begin to enter into the left lane, the second vehicle in the right lane changes lane also, into the very same left lane to pass and broadsides you going at a high rate of speed! (See diagrams.)

DIA Focus Concept: Wait until the left lane coming from the right side is completely clear and no other vehicles are behind the vehicle in the right lane. This gives you a clear opening to the inside left lane. Again, stop yourself from making lane changes close to major intersections. Again, patience is the focus concept here.

The "Lane Change" Intersection Accident (1)

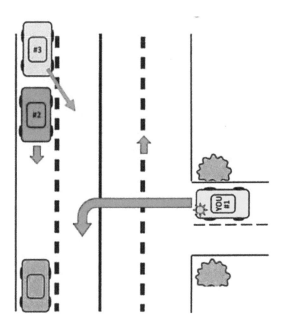

➢ <u>Scenario:</u> You are in Vehicle #1 pulling out to make a left turn into the inside left lane. <u>At the exact same time,</u> Vehicle #3 changes into the same inside left lane.

The "Lane Change" Intersection Accident (2)

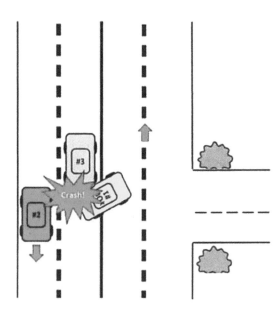

➢ <u>Scenario:</u> You are in Vehicle #1 pulling out to make a left turn into the inside left lane. <u>At the same time,</u> Vehicle #3 changes into the same inside left lane.

➢ <u>Focus concept:</u> Do not pull out until traffic has passed and you are 100 percent sure ALL THE LANES ARE CLEAR!

The "Curves and Hills" Intersection Accident

This accident occurs when Vehicle #2 approaches a hill or curve at an excessive speed. The intersection is just on the other side of the hill. Being Vehicle #1 trying to make a left turn and understanding this is a blind spot DangerZone, you may want to make a right turn instead and go to a safe turnaround.

If you are the vehicle coming up the hill or curve, remember to be aware of losing visibility, and the possibility of vehicles pulling out! Usually there are warning and speed limit signs designating an intersection ahead on the other side of hill. Be aware of these speed limit warning signs also and slow down according to available visibility.

DIA Focus Concept: When approaching curves and hills with blind spots, reduce your speed according to reduced visibility.

IF YOU ARE PULLING OUT FROM CROSSROADS ON OTHER SIDE OF HILL OR CURVE, instead of making a left turn, make a right turn and go to safe turnaround area.

"Hills and Curves" Intersection Accident

> ➤ <u>Scenario:</u> You are approaching a curve or a hill with reduced visibility.
> ➤ <u>Focus Concept</u>: Reduce your speed according to availability and stay in the far-right lane. Detect and Expect.

The "Left Turn—Wheels Are Turned" Intersection Accident

This accident could also fall into the FREAK accident category. You are stopped, preparing to make a left turn on a two-lane or four-lane undivided highway. You have your wheels turned, and suddenly, a vehicle strikes you from behind onto oncoming traffic! CRASH! This accident occurs frequently, and usually the results are fatal or serious injuries due to the speed of the oncoming traffic.

DIA Focus Concept: When stopped in traffic, preparing to make a left turn, NEVER EVER TURN YOUR WHEELS UNTIL YOU BEGIN MAKING THE TURN! Make this a conscious habit! See diagram.

The "Left Turn—Wheels Are Turned" Intersection Accident (1)

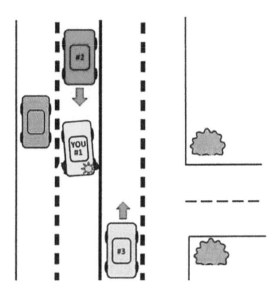

➤ **Scenario:** You are in Vehicle #1, prepared to make a left turn <u>with your wheels turned (incorrect).</u> Vehicle #2 rear-ends you, which forces you to crash with oncoming traffic (Vehicle #3).

The "Left Turn—Wheels Are Turned" Intersection Accident (2)

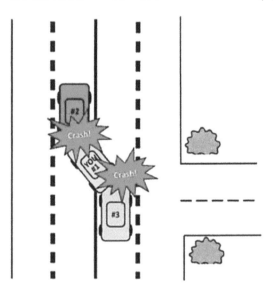

➤ **Scenario:** You are in Vehicle #1, prepared to make a left turn <u>with your wheels turned (incorrect).</u> Vehicle #2 rear-ends you, which forces you to crash with oncoming traffic (Vehicle #3).

➤ **Focus Concept:** Anytime you are stopped in traffic to make a left turn, <u>NEVER EVER turn your wheels until you make the turn!</u>

The "Approaching the Left Turn—Wheels Are Turned Vehicle" Intersection Accident

This is the same type of accident as the previous example, except you are the vehicle approaching and in motion, and not the one making the turn. You are proceeding ahead in the left lane; the oncoming traffic (Vehicle #2) in left lane is stopped, ready to make a left turn. Once you notice the wheels are already turned, your next step is to ensure the traffic behind this vehicle is slowing down also. This is just a proactive move in case the vehicle is struck from behind, sending the vehicle into your lane, striking your vehicle. I would preplan my lane change and go into the right lane ahead of time (I suggest 75–100 feet ahead of intersection). Again, in this situation, it would be a good decision to drive in the right lane. I read of one similar accident in my area, which involved a motorcyclist, killing the motorcyclist and his passenger instantly! This is primarily a survival focus concept when I drive.

DIA Focus Concept: When observing vehicle stopped making a left turn with the wheels turned, be proactive and prepare to move into the right lane when clear (preplan your lane change 75–100 feet ahead of intersection). If the right lane is open, plan to move into it safely. See diagram.

"**Approaching** the Left Turn—Wheels Are Turned Vehicle" Intersection Accident (3)

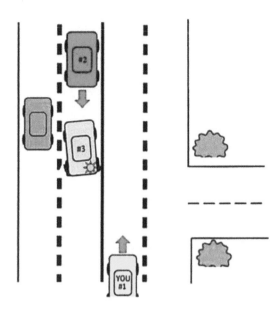

➤ <u>Scenario:</u> You are in Vehicle #1 and you notice that Vehicle #3 has its wheels turned.

"**Approaching** the Left Turn—Wheels Are Turned Vehicle" Intersection Accident (4)

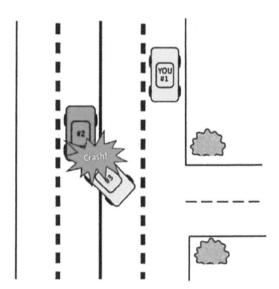

➤ <u>Scenario:</u> You are in Vehicle #1 and you notice that Vehicle #3 has its wheels turned.
➤ <u>Focus Concept</u>: Anytime you detect the wheels turned in this situation, you want to SAFELY PREPLAN and move into your right lane whenever possible to avoid a possible accident. (Safely change lanes ahead of this intersection.)

The "Residential Intersection" Accident

➤ <u>Scenario</u>: There are many intersections in residential areas that have <u>low visibility</u>. Your visibility is reduced, but you continue to drive at the same speed and Vehicle #2 runs the stop sign. You must adjust your speed according to each individual intersection.

Preventing Accident #2:
Lost-Control or Rollover Accidents

- **Lost-control or rollover accidents are increasing and are becoming the number 1 fatal accident with teens. Why?**

In-Vehicle Distractions!

- <u>Texting while driving!</u>
- Eating and drinking
- Playing with Radio/iPods/GPS
- Pets (unsecured)
- Talking and looking at passengers <u>while the wheels are rolling</u>!
- <u>Not well rested</u>
- Improper steering especially on curves
- Speed is too fast for conditions, for example, hydroplaning

LOST-CONTROL or ROLLOVER ACCIDENTS

This type of accident has increased dramatically because of society's change in high-tech communication, with cell phones, texting, laptops, GPS, and other in-vehicle distractions. Other rising causes are speeding during inclement weather.

When I am driving and see someone on the phone, I usually say the same thing out loud: "GET OFF THE PHONE AND DRIVE!" It kills me!

Other key factors that have increased the lost-control type of accident are

Running behind on your driving mission—this automatically makes you an offensive driver! Your tendencies are to make abrupt lane changes and increase your speed. Your decision-making becomes impaired, you become hasty, and this reduces what I call YOUR THOUGHT-PROCESSING TIME. One hasty rash decision can cost your life! Simply put again, be a disciplined 1520 driver.

Excessive speeds during rainstorms = hydroplaning possibilities—Driving too fast has been the cause of lost-control accidents soaring! Reduce to Minus 5, Minus 10 MPH when it is raining to stay in control!

DIA FORMULA FOR POSSIBLE DISASTER

1. EXCESSIVE SPEED + WATER + CUR VES OR HILLS = POSSIBLE DISASTER!

2. ELIMINATE IN-VEHICLE DISTRACTIONS—Completing DIA PRE-DRIVE CHECK AND SETUP ROUTINE is the focus concept here.

Set up your radio/CD/iPod/MP3 to preset station, put away all items, and eliminate any loose articles in your vehicle. Be organized!

Eliminate eating, reading, texting, being on cell phone, and changing radio stations while the wheels are rolling.

If you have pets, you must ensure they do not block your vision or impair your steering. If having a pet in your vehicle is a habit, you are creating a possible in-vehicle distraction that could lead to a serious accident. If you see these drivers with a pet in the front seat, do your best to let them drive away as soon as possible.

*When other passengers are in your vehicle, speak to them without having to look at them. Focus on the road. This has created many rear-end or striking-fixed-object accidents.

DIA Focus Concept:

WHEN THE WHEELS ARE ROLLING, YOU CAN'T BE LOOKING DOWN, TEXTING, OR LOOKING AT ANY PASSENGERS! AND MAINTAIN A SAFE SPEED WHEN IT'S RAINING!

3. KNOW ALL YOUR LANE ENDINGS- As mentioned earlier in lane strategies module, a complete knowledge of where each lane ends at major intersections will help you avoid making abrupt lane changes, possible swerving, and lost-control of your vehicle. You should be aware of all signs giving you the lane endings.

4. IMPROVE CELL PHONE OR TEXTING DISCIPLINE

Learn and make it a disciplined habit to pull over to a safe spot when receiving a phone call if you need to answer call. If not, let the caller leave a message and you can hear it later when at a safe place. ALSO GET HANDS-FREE SYSTEM!

I have noticed an improvement in more people pulling over and talking on the cell phone. Just remember the days when we did not have cell phones; we would pull off the road and go to a payphone. Now, you can just simply pull off to a safe spot. Again, make this a disciplined habit. Get off the phone and drive! <u>NO TEXTING WHILE THE WHEELS ARE ROLLING!</u>

5. ARE YOU WELL RESTED? Only you, the driver, know the answer to this question. You must be responsible for knowing if you are capable of driving in a manner to protect yourself and loved ones when you get behind the wheel of a vehicle.

Countless people have been killed in vehicle accidents because of a driver falling asleep and losing control! On long trips, you must take steps to eliminate falling asleep at the wheel. On these trips, the safer decision would be to leave the following morning and not drive overnight (unless well rested). This eliminates the danger of falling asleep at the wheel!

NOTE: Driving when not well rested is more dangerous than driving under the influence!

These are the factors and focus concepts you must be knowledgeable of and disciplined to prevent the lost-control-type accident. And, also be disciplined in securing your seatbelt.

6. STEERING HABITS—BE DISCIPLINED IN PROPER STEERING HABITS

In my driving approximately 1,000 miles a week on my route, which had many hills and curves, it was imperative that I always had complete control of the steering wheel. I would think to myself, "If I have a blowout right this second going around this curve, I must have both hands properly on steering wheel, or I will surely flip!" This is a critical fundamental habit when driving. You hear about the driver who overcorrected, many times they only had one hand on the wheel when they lost control.

DIA Focus Concept: Become a DIA Certified Teen Driver with disciplined steering habits and <u>stay in control every second that you drive.</u>

The Rollover Accidents

The Rollover accident—I would classify this accident much like the lost-control type of accident. This module will discuss the root causes of the rollover accident, how to stay in control and eliminate any of these root causes.

The main root causes in this type of accident are as follows:

Departing late to destination (not following the 1520 rule) can result in speeding around a curve and rolling over!

Not completing D1A's Pre-Drive Check and Setup Routine (which increases in-vehicle distractions), not being well rested, and improper steering habits increase rollover risks.

Imagine what would happen if you were going around a curve and had a blowout!

Are you ready and able to control your vehicle? The answer needs to be yes! This is especially for curvy highways. Proper steering positioning at 10 and 2 is the key to consistent control.

In-vehicle distractions are the #1 root causes for rollover accidents (texting, loose articles in vehicle, pets in vehicle, looking at others while talking, eating, and looking down or at your passengers while the wheels are rolling). Eliminate distractions, which will eliminate rollovers!

Darting Wildlife! You must be focused on the road and stay alert looking for wildlife in all directions. The DangerZone in some rural areas are lots of trees lining both sides of the road, with the possibility of wildlife darting out! My focus concept again is "Minus 5, Minus 10 MPH" and scan constantly in all areas. This is how I drive in these areas with lots of deer. I am continually scanning for deer grazing on both sides of the road and adjusting speed accordingly.

Excessive speed on curves—Focus Concept: <u>Look further ahead</u> on curves and <u>maintain a safe speed as you enter a curve</u>.

All it takes is a quick distraction that takes your eyes off the road. Next, you find yourself off the road, and the normal reaction is to quickly get back on the road. This overcompensation usually leads to losing control and rolling the vehicle over!

As mentioned before, every driving mission must be met with disciplined habits, and by following the 1520 rule (the solution for eliminating speeding) and the Pre-Drive Check and Setup Routine (the solution for eliminating distractions), the two main root causes have been eliminated.

Tire marks are the results of distracted and/or high-speed drivers.

Focus Concepts

- <u>ELIMINATE ALL DISTRACTIONS!</u>
- Proper control of steering at all times, especially on curves and down hills (blowout)
- <u>Be well rested</u> before driving
- <u>Adjust speed according to inclement weather conditions.</u> (Eliminate hydroplaning possibilities!) <u>Minus 5, Minus 10 MPH!</u>
- Be <u>100 percent focused and in control from point A to point B</u>!

Preventing Accident #3: The Head-ons

- **Head-on** accidents are increasing! Why?
- Seventy-four million elderly baby boomers are still driving.
- <u>**Root causes:**</u>
  - **Poor vision**
  - **Medications**
  - **Health problems**
  - **Unfamiliar roads**
  - **Wrong-way drivers**
  - **Distractions**
  - **Passing out**
  - **Suicides**

Feb. 9, 2014. Officials investigate the scene of a multiple vehicle accident where 6 people were killed on the westbound Pomona Freeway in Diamond Bar, Calif., on Sunday. Authorities say a wrong-way driver caused the pre-dawn crash that left six people dead. (AP/San Gabriel Valley Tribune,Watchara Phomicinda)

THE HEAD-ONS

The "Crossed the Centerline!" Head-On

This accident has become more prevalent because of several factors: an aging society, drivers dozing off, the high-tech era (i.e., cell phones, GPS, laptops, CD/MP3) and other in-vehicle distractions. How many times have you read in a newspaper or heard in TV newscasts, "The driver crossed the centerline"? The other driver was not detecting and expecting and therefore was reactive versus proactive, which was too late! Head-on collisions usually result in very serious injuries or death that can happen in a split second!

This module will teach you some very simple prevention and life-saving steps. You or I could have easily been one of these stats. I call this "being at the wrong place at the wrong time!" The number one reason causing head-on accidents is one driver crossing the centerline. The root causes are usually (1) driver fell asleep; (2) driver had heart attack or medical problem causing driver to pass out; (3) driver distracted by in-vehicle distraction (playing with radio or looking at passengers while talking) and lost control; (4) driver had a blowout; (5) driver driving under the influence of alcohol or drugs, (6) driver dropped article and tried to pick it up off floor, taking eyes off road and turning steering wheel at the same time!

As a DIA Certified Teen Driver, you want to be prepared for any of these possibilities. When I make the decision to be in the left lane, I understand and execute the following: (1) always try to leave an opening into the right lane (by being staggered/offset), and (2) so important that I am prepared and expecting the oncoming vehicle to possibly cross the centerline! Should the vehicle begin to cross the line, being proactive, I will simply change lanes without hesitation. You must drive expecting this possibility when in the left lane.

Review the following diagrams and make the proper decisions when you are a left-lane driver. Again, when I get in the left lane, it is usually to pass the vehicle in the right lane. Whenever possible, I try to pass when there is no oncoming traffic if on an undivided four-lane highway. The reason is to avoid being blocked in, or the vehicle in right lane changes, or weaves into the left lane.

The "Crossing the Centerline" Head-On

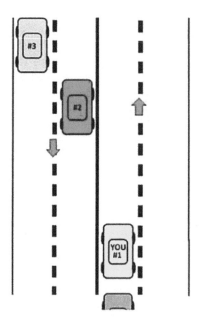

> **Scenario:** You are in the left lane, and you notice <u>the oncoming vehicle is crossing the centerline!</u>

The "Crossing the Centerline" Head-On

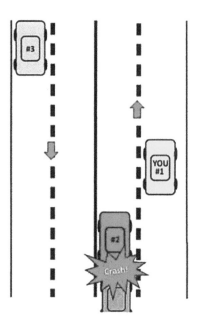

> **Scenario:** You are in the left lane, and you notice <u>the oncoming vehicle is crossing the centerline.</u>
> **Focus Concept:** BY BEING <u>STAGGERED and PROACTIVE, you simply slide</u> into the right lane to avoid any possible Head-on collision.

The "Wrong-Way Driver" Head-On

Four-Lane Divided Highway/Frontage Roads/
Bridges/Curves/Overpasses

This is what I would consider a freak accident also. This head-on occurs on four-lane divided (with a median) highways with curves, overpasses/bridges, and frontage roads. Here is a scenario regarding this accident.

It is nighttime and about a mile ahead, Vehicle #2 is on a road that crosses the highway you are driving on. Being new to the area or under the influence, the driver makes a left turn on this four-lane divided highway. Thinking it is only a two-lane road, the driver goes into what he thinks is the right lane. He is traveling the wrong way! And if you are in the left lane, you will not know this until you reach the crest of the hill or curve. CRASH! It is too late! There is a higher frequency of this type of accident with drivers who are under the influence. Usually this accident occurs on weekends late at night or in the wee, early morning hours.

When driving at night, or daytime for that matter, <u>I do not go over bridges, overpasses, hills, or around a curve in the left lane</u> on a four-lane divided highway for this very reason.

If you do, make sure you are staggered and prepared to change into middle or right lane. Please look at correct and incorrect steps in the diagrams below. Analyze any four-lane divided highways where you drive where there are hills and curves. Ask yourself, "Is this an area where someone could drive the wrong way? What's my lane strategy plan to avoid a possible wrong way head-on?" The possibility would be higher at night, but I would drive in the right lane or middle lane (if three lanes on divided highway) until I cleared the hill or curve. I have an area with this possibility about two miles from my home. This is how I try to drive. See Diagrams.

The Wrong-Way Head-On (Hills and Curves)

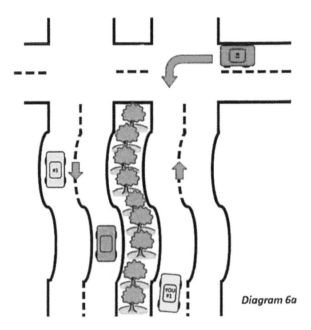

Diagram 6a

> ➤ **Scenario: This is <u>four lanes divided with a median, and Vehicle #2 driver accidentally turns left into the wrong lane, thinking that it's only two lanes!</u>**
>   - ✓ If you are driving in the left lane coming over a hill or curve, you are more likely to have a wrong-way head-on collision, <u>especially late at night and during weekends</u>.
>   - ✓ <u>Statistics</u>: In one year recently, there were 260 wrong-way head-on collisions, resulting in 360 fatalities! <u>DO NOT be one of these statistics!</u>

The Wrong-Way Head-On (Hills and Curves)

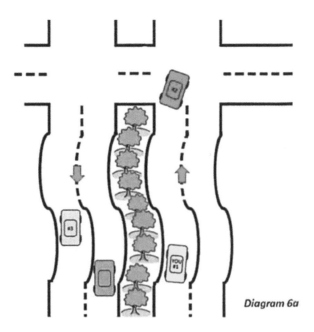

Diagram 6a

> ➤ **Scenario: This is <u>four lanes divided with a median, and Vehicle #2 driver accidentally turns left into the wrong lane, thinking that it's only two lanes!</u>**
>> ✓ If you are driving in the left lane coming over a hill or curve, you are more likely to have a wrong-way head-on collision, <u>especially late at night and during weekends</u>.

The Wrong-Way Head-On (Hills and Curves)

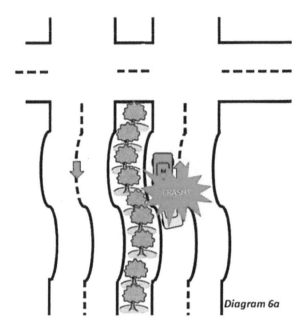

Diagram 6a

➤ **Scenario: This is four lanes divided with a median, and Vehicle #2 driver accidentally turns left into the wrong lane, thinking that it's only two lanes.**

    ✓ If you are driving in the left lane coming over a hill or curve, you are more likely to have a wrong-way head-on collision, <u>especially late at night and during weekends</u>.

➤ **Focus Concept:** Avoid driving in left lane when approaching curves, hills, and overpasses. On frontage roads, the right lane is preferred. <u>On six-lane divided highways, the middle lane is recommended.</u>

The "Passing in Left Lane on Four-Lane Undivided Highway" Head-On

Here is the scenario covered in Strategic Lane Driving Plan: I am on a four-lane undivided highway. I am in the right lane, and traffic is slow. I make the decision to go into the left lane and preplan on passing the vehicle in the right lane. I do not attempt to pass until there is no oncoming traffic. This is how I try to drive. If I begin to pass the vehicle and the vehicle in the right lane weaves or changes into the left lane, this would instantly push me directly head-on into the oncoming traffic!

There was an accident on a four-lane undivided road in my city, where the driver in the right lane failed to signal and pushed the vehicle that was in the left lane directly into oncoming traffic, killing that driver instantly!

This is how many people have become head-on statistics on four-lane undivided roads. The focus concept is not to get yourself boxed in! If the vehicle changes lanes when there is no oncoming traffic, I would go across the centerline, knowing there are no vehicles coming toward me. There are a couple of four-lane undivided stretches where I avoid driving in the left lane altogether because of sharp curves and all the head-on possibilities. I intentionally stay back when seeing the situation like in this picture below.

DIA Focus Concept: When passing in the left lane on a four-lane undivided road, attempt to pass when there is no oncoming traffic whenever possible. Your mindset is to survive on these types of highways.

Understanding Lane Strategies—"Passing in Left Lane" Head-on

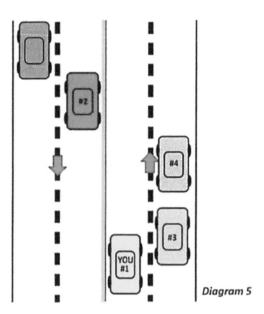

Diagram 5

➢ **Scenario: You need to pass a vehicle with oncoming traffic and undivided lanes.**
  ✓ If you need to pass a vehicle, remain in the right lane or staggered until all oncoming traffic has passed by, before changing lanes to avoid a possible head-on collision should a car accidentally cross the centerline.
  ✓ Also, be prepared should Vehicle #3 decide to change into the inside lane at the same time you do.

Understanding Lane Strategies—"Passing in Left Lane" Head-on

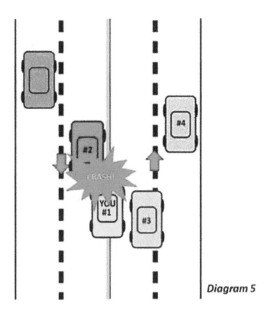

Diagram 5

- ➢ <u>**Scenario**</u>**: You need to pass a vehicle with oncoming traffic and undivided lanes.**
    - ✓ If you need to pass a vehicle, remain in the right lane or staggered until all oncoming traffic has passed by, before changing lanes to avoid a possible head-on collision should a car accidentally cross the centerline.
    - ✓ Also, be prepared should Vehicle #3 decide to change into the inside lane at the same time you do.

The "Sharp Curve, Wrong Lane!" Head-On

(Rural Two-Lane Road)

On a rural two-lane road with a sharp curve, the main focus concepts are to maintain a safe speed and stay in the proper lane when approaching the curve. The tendencies when driving on these sharp curvy roads are to cut too sharply or swing out too wide.

In my driving duties, at least two or three times a week, I would encounter this situation where the oncoming traffic coming around the curve would be in my lane! I did see a few surprised drivers! Being pro-active, I followed the habits of staying properly in my lane, slowing down (on some curves, almost coming to a stop), and tapping my horn prior to entering the curve.

DIA Focus Concept: On sharp curves with two lanes, Stay in your lane! Reduce speed accordingly and tap horn prior to entering curve.

Two-Lane Sharp Curve

Diagram 7

➢ **Scenario: In a two-lane sharp curve, Vehicle #2 is making a sharp turn into your lane.**
　✓　You should approach curves with a tap of your horn and hug the right side of your lane safely.

➢ **Focus Concept: Tap horn when approaching blind curves and be prepared for oncoming traffic making a sharp turn into your lane.**

Preventing Accident #4: Striking Fixed Objects or Hitting Others in Rear

- Distracted driver fatalities up 4 percent—why?
- <u>Texting</u>! Taking eyes off the road <u>when the wheels are rolling</u>!
- **Tailgating**, high-speed highways! (**Being a Groupie**!)
- **Dropping Articles! BENDING!**
- ➢ <u>FOCUS CONCEPTS:</u> STAY AWAY FROM THE GROUPIES!
- ➢ **When the wheels are rolling, <u>you can't be looking down</u>, <u>TEXTING, or looking at your passengers</u>!**

STRIKING FIXED OBJECTS or HITTING OTHERS IN REAR

Imagine you're driving about 50–60 mph and you look down at your radio or console, and the vehicle in front of you stops at the same time! The force of this impact will surely result in very serious injuries or even fatalities. You may have seen this type of accident in your town or city. These accidents are also becoming more frequent, again because of a busy society and the increased distractions. GPS screens, cell phones, laptops, playing with radio/iPod, and many other in-vehicle distractions—these have greatly increased our lack of focus on the driving mission. This must change!

As discussed earlier, the <u>DIA Pre-Drive Check and Setup Routine</u> will eliminate any in-vehicle distractions as you complete your driving mission.

Please go back to review all the steps in the DIA Pre-Drive Check and Setup Routine.

DIA Focus Concepts: "WHEN THE WHEELS ARE ROLLING, YOU CAN'T BE LOOKING DOWN, TEXTING, OR LOOKING AT ANY PASSENGERS" and "STAY AWAY FROM THE GROUPIES (all those bunched-up drivers)!"

These are the DIA focus concepts when you find yourself driving on your interstate or toll roads (high-speed roads). All traffic is driving 65–70 mph and bunched up together (a.k.a. groupies). This is a recipe for a possible multiple-vehicle collision we see on our morning or evening commutes.

My tip-off is when I notice several vehicles ahead repeatedly stepping on their brakes. I start to protect my space and back off immediately.

We have all heard this in the news or read in the paper: a four-car or ten-car pile-up.

You must keep a safe distance from the vehicle ahead of yours and DON'T BE A GROUPIE!

When receiving a phone call, develop the habit of pulling over to a safe place as we mentioned earlier. Also, leaving in sufficient time (**the 1520 rule**) will help you avoid possibility of tailgating and pushing too hard.

Again, avoid trying to pick up any dropped articles while the vehicle is in motion.

The Continual-Cruising Eggshell

This may sound hokey, but what I call the Continual-Cruising Eggshell is so helpful and a preventative, proactive focus concept when executed properly. It has worked for me. I drive with this focus concept, and my trainees have said they like this concept also.

Let us look at the egg: the yolk is toward the back part of the egg; there is one side of the egg that is longer than the other. Now, let us make your car like the yolk of the egg and put an imaginary shell around it. The longest part of the shell is going to be in front of your vehicle. You always want to keep a safe space ahead of your vehicle, and this imaginary shell should never be broken!

Establish the habit of <u>looking ahead</u> of the vehicle you are following. By doing this, you are prepared to protect your space in the event the vehicle ahead of the one you are following hits their brakes abruptly. This focus concept will also protect you when stopped in traffic; you leave enough space that allows you to pull out in the event the vehicle behind you may strike you in the rear! <u>It also helps me eliminate abrupt stops and avoid wearing out my brakes.</u>

See diagrams.

DIA Focus Concept: Protect your eggshell continually. <u>Don't crack the eggshell</u>!

The Continual-Cruising Eggshell

- When driving, <u>keep the protection in front of your vehicle similar to the longest part of the eggshell, which protects its yolk.</u>

Focus Concept: Always drive to protect your vehicle and you with the Continual-Cruising Eggshell focus concept. DON'T CRACK THE EGGSHELL!

You Can Prevent Being Rear-Ended!

Ninety-five percent of drivers would say, if you are stopped in traffic and get rear-ended, there is nothing you could have done to prevent it. People have told me there was no way I could have prevented it, since I was stopped. <u>The prevention of this accident is before you come to a complete stopped position.</u> I will show you how you can prevent being rear-ended.

Now just follow me on this so you can prevent ever being rear-ended in the future. Scenarios: You are driving and notice the green light ahead turns yellow, then red. As a DIA-trained driver, you begin slowing down, and <u>the focus concept is to automatically check your mirrors to see any vehicles behind you as you start coasting in.</u> Now, there are two different scenarios that can happen.

Scenario 1: There are no vehicles behind you; therefore, you coast toward the light, and <u>you are the first vehicle approaching the light, so you simply save a space ahead of the crosswalk. Continue to check your mirrors until you see a vehicle approaching behind you. *If the vehicle is not slowing down, you may need to blast your horn and drive forward since you left sufficient space ahead for this very reason.</u>

Scenario 2: <u>You are the second vehicle</u> approaching a red light. You see the vehicle behind you, and in this situation, the focus concept is the same: to <u>perform an AUTOMATIC MIRROR CHECK and protect the space ahead of you, by controlling the vehicle behind you. Leave sufficient space between you and the vehicle in front of you in case you have to pull out!</u> This will eventually become a very important discipline. See diagrams.

People who have been rear-ended before have learned to make this a habit and are more conscious of these situations. This is a habit that needs to be practiced and perfected. <u>When I drive, this is one of my biggest fears, being rear-ended by the distracted drivers on our highways.</u>

Avoid Being Rear-Ended: No Vehicles Behind You

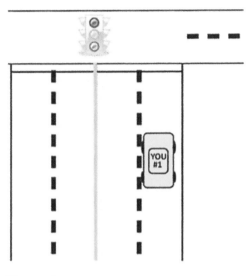

Diagram 2a

➢ <u>Scenario:</u> **The light turns red; you are <u>the first vehicle</u> approaching the stop light.**
  ✓ Automatically check rear-view mirror for approaching vehicles from behind.
  ✓ If you notice that there are no vehicles behind you, save one car length of space in front of your vehicle should a vehicle approach too fast behind you.
  ✓ If a vehicle is coming too fast, <u>immediately blast your horn and move forward to prevent being rear-ended</u>.

Avoid Being Rear-Ended: Vehicles Behind You

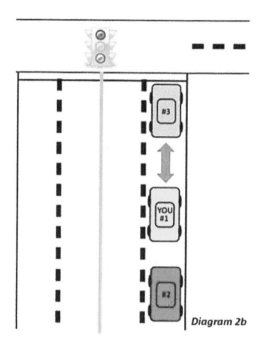

Diagram 2b

➤ **Scenario: You are <u>the second vehicle</u> approaching a red light.**
 ✓ <u>Automatically check rear-view mirror</u> for approaching vehicles from behind you.
 ✓ As you approach the vehicle in front of you (#3), slow down by tapping your brakes to control the vehicle behind you (#2).
 ✓ Protect the space between you and the vehicle in front of you should you need to move out.
➤ **Focus Concept: <u>Protect the space</u> in front of you <u>by controlling</u> the vehicle behind you.**

Preventing Accident #5: Pedestrians, Bicyclists, and Motorcyclists

➢ <u>Fatalities in Texas 2017:</u>
- Pedestrians – 614
- Bicyclists – 57
- Motorcyclists – 501

➢ GHSA (Gov't Highway Safety Admin.) projected a 10 percent increase.
➢ A majority occur at night on major highways (**1.7 percent possible suicides—GHSA**).
➢ Fifty percent occur when crossing or entering intersections.

Our life can change in <u>ONE SPLIT SECOND</u>!

➢ <u>When you see a BICYCLIST or MOTORCYCLIST in your side mirror or rear-view mirror, be aware of their position UNTIL YOU OR THEY TURN OFF AND GO SEPARATE WAYS!</u>

<u>FOCUS CONCEPT</u>:

➢ <u>ACTIVATE YOUR NIGHT VISION!</u>
➢ <u>DETECT AND EXPECT</u> where pedestrians may be and communicate.

PEDESTRIANS, BICYCLISTS, and MOTORCYCLISTS

When driving, our lives can change in one split second! Yes, this is true when it comes to driving with many more pedestrians, bicyclists, and motorcyclists on our roads today.

As we discussed in the module "Analyze Your Area," this is a good place to start by learning about the demographics of where you live and drive the most. Does your area have a large amount of people who commute by walking? What about bicyclists and motorcyclists—are there many of them in your area?

Pedestrian fatalities from 2005 to 2014 have averaged 4,610 pedestrians killed on our nation's highways (from GHSA stats)! Of these pedestrian fatalities, 1.7 percent have been classified as possible suicides (GHSA stats). God forbid, but if you were to hit a pedestrian, DO NOT LEA VE THE SCENE! After investigation, they may have been in a suicidal state. They find out the person had just lost their job or was recently divorced or in financial trouble, so they just darted out into the highway! This would most likely be judged as a non-preventable accident.

The DIA focus concept of "activating your night vision" must be an ongoing habit throughout your night driving mission. DIA says, "Look for objects that do not give off a reflection!" Your lights will shine sufficiently to spot people walking at night, but you must be looking for them! It also has been reported that one third of pedestrians and one fifth of bicyclists are under the influence! Many pedestrians are texting while walking or wearing headphones with the music blasting away! You must stay observant.

In residential areas, the pedestrian fatalities have been primarily children who were in front of a parked vehicle and darted across the street! It is your responsibility as a licensed driver to ensure driving within the posted speed limits and scan for these possible situations.

Bicyclists are also increasing on our roads. You need to focus primarily on communicating with them in a proper manner. Using your horn may be necessary, but it must not be too far away, where the bicyclist cannot hear you, and not too close, where you may scare them into your path. Keep your eyes on the road when the wheels are rolling!

This is the same situation regarding motorcyclists. The focus concept is, when you see a motorcyclist or bicyclist in your mirror, be aware of their position until you or they turn off and go your separate ways! Please understand, it is harder to judge the speed of a motorcyclist when they are approaching the intersection from your left or right. Focus Concept: Take the extra second, or seconds, to judge their approaching speed.

Preventing Accident #6: Night Driving Accidents

> ## ROOT CAUSES:
> - Decreased visibility!
> - Drivers under the influence!
> - Unfamiliarity with area!
> - Speeding with lower visibility and in inclement weather!
> - In city areas where there are lots of pedestrians and pedi-cyclist!
> - <u>Chicago Tribune article</u>: **25 percent of drivers on the road are causing 50 percent of night driving fatalities!**

NIGHT DRIVING ACCIDENTS

When I drive at night, I understand the following: my visibility is reduced, and there are a few people out there who have just left happy hour on the road! These are the times I am really focused when approaching an intersection with a green light and making sure all the cross traffic stops. You need to have an increased awareness of this when driving at night.

When my sons were teens and getting ready to drive somewhere at night, I would always give them safety tips. For night driving, I would say the following: "Look for cars without lights," or "Activate your night vision", or "Minus 5, Minus 10." The "Minus 5, Minus 10" referred to reducing your speed at least 5 to 10 miles per hour at night, especially in those rural areas with lots of wildlife and reduced visibility. Most highway speed limit signs already have the reduced night speed limits indicated.

Here is a scenario of a night driving accident resulting in a fatality. The driver is leaving home after dusk and comes to a stop sign intersection. He looks left and sees the car lights far away, then looks right and sees the car lights far away, then checks left again. He pulls out, and CRASH! The vehicle that hit him (maybe a happy hour attendee) going 60 miles per hour did not have his lights on!

The solution for preventing this accident is simple and must become a habit for you. First, let us look at the root cause of this accident. When the driver looked left, he saw the lights of the vehicle coming from the left about a block away. Looking right, he sees the other vehicle's lights about a block away. The driver's vision was drawn out to the lights of these vehicles, and he never saw the vehicle without lights on that was very close upon him, coming at high rate of speed! And this closest area is the real DangerZone!

THE NIGHT DRIVING PULLOUT AT INTERSECTIONS focus concept is to scan in, then scan out in both directions, and look for any vehicle without lights or anything not giving off a reflection! Try this habit, practice it, and share it with your friends and loved ones. Remember, the DangerZone is the cross traffic closest to where you are pulling out from. See diagram.

I call this focus concept IN AND OUT NIGHT VISION.

Also, the other focus concept for night driving is ACTIVATE YOUR NIGHT VISION. By looking for vehicles without their lights on, you will see those vehicles without lights on, also bicyclists and pedestrians sooner by activating your night vision and prevent a possible serious accident.

When driving on dark rural highways at night, I use my high beams whenever there is no oncoming traffic. It gives me a better of view of any possible wildlife on the shoulder of the highway and helps me negotiate a safer speed rounding curves.

In-and-Out Night Vision

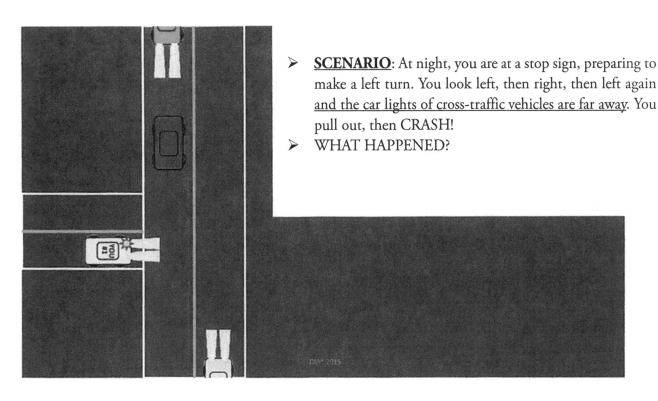

> **SCENARIO**: At night, you are at a stop sign, preparing to make a left turn. You look left, then right, then left again <u>and the car lights of cross-traffic vehicles are far away</u>. You pull out, then CRASH!
> WHAT HAPPENED?

In-and-Out Night Vision

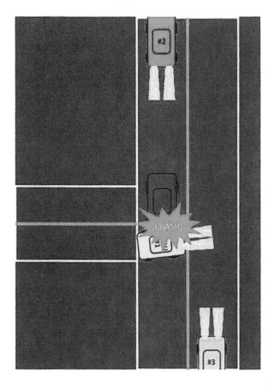

> **SCENARIO**: At night, you are stopped at an intersection, preparing to make a left turn. You look left, then right, then left again and the car lights of cross-traffic vehicles are far away. You pull out, then CRASH!
> What happened?
> <u>Your vision was drawn out</u> toward the lights far away and you did not see the car coming without lights!

FOCUS CONCEPTS:

> <u>ACTIVATE YOUR NIGHT VISION!</u>
> <u>FOLLOW "IN-AND-OUT" NIGHT VISION FOCUS CONCEPT.</u>
> <u>MINUS 5, MINUS 10 MPH.</u>
> FOCUS ON PEDESTRIANS and anything not giving off a reflection.

Activate Your Night Vision
—Looking for vehicles without their lights on
(see the vehicle circled)

Left Lane, Middle Lane, or Right Lane— Which Is the Safest Lane at Night?

When driving at night on a four-lane undivided highway, I usually drive in the right lane, but I follow the "Minus 5, Minus 10 MPH" focus concept, being aware of possible pedestrians walking or vehicles stopped on shoulder of road. Also, if it is late at night, there is the possibility of drivers under the influence. So, I up my game being extremely alert and focused. You must also focus and drive this way.

When people ask, "What is the safest lane to drive in?" My response is "Any lane is safe as long as you understand what possible accidents could arise from being in that particular lane, and you take the necessary preventative precautions when driving in the lane you are in."

As stated before, if you are in the left lane, your mission is that you try to be staggered/offset, with an opening as much as possible into the right lane. I try to drive to minimize my lane changes as much as possible on any routes driven.

Remember, late at night, going over a hill or curved highway on a four-lane divided highway, I avoid the left lane! I take the right lane; again, if on a six-lane divided highway, the middle lane is my best option. If I am in the right lane (day or night), I stay alert for pedestrians or vehicles stopped over the crest or around the curve.

Preventing Accident #7: The Freak Accidents

These are totally unexpected, catching a driver off guard!

THE FREAK ACCIDENTS

In the past forty-plus years, I have heard, read, or seen many types of accidents that I classify as freak accidents. Like I have said, my main vision, or goal with this book is that KNOWLEDGE = PREVENTION AND SURVIVAL!

This module will give you information helping you to eliminate being in a vulnerable situation. Some of these accidents you may have heard of. And if it happened to someone else, it could happen to you or me!

When I drive, I try to do all that is possible to avoid being in any of these types of freak accidents. Again, share this information with your family and friends. I know teaching this to others is hard because everyone already thinks they are good drivers, and it is kind of a boring topic.

It is my hope everyone who drives a vehicle will read and receive what is being taught in this book. My friends, family, and those who have received my training have been transformed in how they approach and execute the DIA curriculum. Here are some examples of several freak accidents.

Following Machinery—Odd Equipment

Here is one freak accident that happened in Texas. A vehicle was following a large flatbed tractor trailer carrying a forklift on the back of trailer. The forklift was higher than the cab of the tractor trailer! When the driver went under the bridge, the forklift struck the bridge! The forklift came off the trailer and fell on top of the vehicle following behind! The driver and passengers were all killed instantly!

The **focus concept** here is to avoid following these types of vehicles <u>whenever possible</u>. Also, avoid following anyone pulling a personal trailer, moving trailer, boats, or other machinery <u>whenever possible</u>. Preplan your lane change and pass these types of vehicles <u>whenever possible</u>.

Avoid Following Vehicles with Heavy Machinery, Landscape Equipment, Movers, Open Trailers whenever possible

Accident Scenario: A vehicle was following a tractor trailer carrying a forklift. **The forklift did not clear the overpass and came off the trailer, killing the occupants in the vehicle behind the tractor trailer!**

DANGER!

Following a landscaper can give dangerous results as debris or other equipment can fly out and hit your car, or you!

> **FOCUS CONCEPT**: Avoid following these types of vehicles whenever possible, by either changing lanes or passing them.

Cement Trucks

There have been numerous accidents in which a vehicle was smashed by a cement truck toppling over when making a turn. When empty, cement trucks have a very high center of gravity; therefore, if going too fast on a turn, it can easily roll over!

*With double left turning lanes, your prevention focus concept is to become staggered/offset immediately as you turn, avoiding being in any position to get crushed by a toppling cement truck!

Open Trailers

Following someone who is moving and has an open trailer with furniture or other miscellaneous articles that can come loose or blowout of the trailer is not a good habit.

They usually drive in the right lane. Once you find yourself behind these types of vehicles, preplan your lane change, and pass when safe to avoid any possible accident.

There was an accident where an ax fell out from a landscaper's open trailer. The ax crashed into the windshield of the vehicle following the landscaper! The passenger in the front seat narrowly escaped a very serious injury. See picture.

DIA Focus Concept: Avoid following vehicles with open trailers, furniture, landscape equipment, and those carrying machinery equipment whenever possible. Preplan all lane changes.

Missed Exit or Turnaround Accident

You are on a two-lane rural highway or a four-lane undivided highway. In this scenario, you missed the crossroads and pulled over to the shoulder, then glanced in the mirror. Next, you proceed to make a U-turn, then CRASH!

You did not get the complete view of all the traffic by just relying on your mirrors. The correct focus concept prevention steps are to continue driving to the next crossroads, turn onto the crossroads, and then make your left turn back safely onto the main highway. You now have a complete field of vision to make your left turn.

DIA Focus Concept: Do not just rely on mirrors—go to a safe crossroads and obtain a complete field of vision, then make a safe left turn.

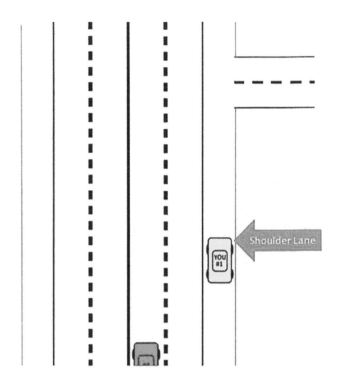

Unsafe Turnaround

> **Scenario:** You missed your exit, you pull over to the shoulder lane, you look in your mirrors, and you don't see any cars coming. You proceed to make a U-turn. CRASH!

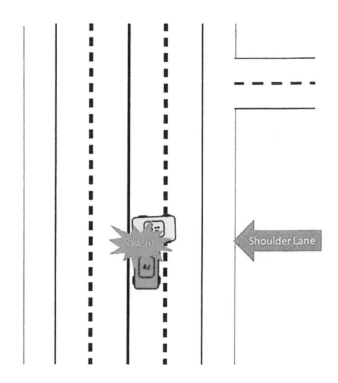

Unsafe Turn Around

> **Scenario: You missed your exit, you pull over to the shoulder lane, you look in your mirrors, and you don't see any cars coming. You proceed to make a U-turn. CRASH!**

> You did not get <u>a complete look by relying only on your mirrors</u>!

<u>Focus Concept:</u>

> <u>Instead, proceed to the next crossroads and make a safe turnaround.</u>

The Two Most Frequent Accidents—Backing and Parking Lot Backing Accidents

Backing Accidents

If you follow these fundamental focus concepts, you will prevent the possibility of being in a parking lot backing accident. <u>First and foremost, you want to avoid having to back up altogether!</u> (See photo.) <u>If you do need to back up, you want to do it prior to doing anything else.</u> When having to back up, check both mirrors and back up slowly and immediately. Next, and very important, do not over-back! <u>OVER-BACKING is the biggest cause of backing accidents in parking lots.</u> *Note: Back up just enough to set your vehicle out.

DIA focus concepts for preventing Backing accidents:

1. **Eliminate backing whenever possible**
2. **Back up prior to next task—do all backing first**
3. **Check mirrors and tap horn always!**
4. **Back up cautiously and urgently**
5. **Do not OVERBACK! Just back up enough to get you out**

The Two Most Frequent Accidents: Backing and Parking Lots (1)

Backing

Why is it a frequent accident?

- **Over-backing** is the #1 cause!
- **Not physically checking** the rear of your vehicle well enough, especially in residential areas. **Toddlers in residential areas: "Daddy is going to the grocery store!"**
- **Not communicating** by tapping your horn. It's free, and it makes others aware that you are backing up
- All backing accidents are avoidable!

The Two Most Frequent Accidents: Backing and Parking Lots (2)

Focus Concepts:

- Avoid backing altogether.
- **Physically check** the rear of vehicle (toddlers in residentials)
- **Communicate** by tapping your horn.
- **Minimize backing distance**—just enough to get you out

Backing Toddler Accident

One of the most important modules in this book to me is "Analyze Your Area." It is a very short and simple module, but it covers knowing all about the immediate area where you live. On your block right now, do you have neighbors with small children or toddlers? If the answer is yes, you need to always follow the DIA focus concept of **physically checking the rear anytime you back out of a driveway! If you have small children or toddlers yourself, this information is critical.** We have all read of the terrible tragedy where the parent runs over their own child when backing out of the driveway!

Let's review a scenario of how this could happen. <u>Follow me closely on this</u>. The husband and wife are talking and saying, "Daddy is going to the store." <u>The toddler hears this and sneaks out of the home, wanting to go also, but Daddy did not notice the child following him. The toddler gets behind the vehicle and is struck by the car backing out!</u> If you have children or your neighbors do, you must always execute the focus concept of <u>physically</u> checking rear area prior to backing. You must make this a habit along with two short horn beeps.

DIA Focus Concept: ALWAYS PHYSICALLY CHECK THE REAR OF YOUR VEHICLE BEFORE BACKING OUT AND TAP YOUR HORN.

When backing,

Tap your horn and physically check the rear area of your vehicle.

Children in Residentials

When driving in residential areas, your main focus concepts are maintaining a safe speed and continual visual scanning. <u>You should be scanning for children who may be behind parked vehicles or hidden behind other objects</u>. Increased horn usage is also recommended. Look at the diagram/photos below and follow the DIA focus concepts when driving in residential areas. Remember, you must be in control at all times; therefore, avoid dropping your guard in these residential areas. All it takes is a couple of seconds of being distracted to change many people's lives!

DIA focus concepts in residential areas:

Maintain a safe speed.

Maintain continual visual scans.

Look for children near blind spots, in front and around vehicles.

Safe Speed in Residentials and Scanning for Children

Parking Lot Accidents

To me, parking lots are just one big DangerZone! Why? Primarily because there are many vehicles in one condensed area; they are moving in and out, backing up, and many are not driving at safe speeds!

I am sure you have encountered someone driving in the parking lot who was traveling at an excessive speed. Your main focus concepts will be simple. You must maintain a safe speed. You must be like what I call "the lion in the jungle." The lion in the jungle is constantly being observant (detecting) and scanning all areas for the hunter that may kill him (expecting)!

Your objective is to scan for those moving in and out, scan for backup lights, and people walking out behind vehicles. Finally, use your horn and communicate as needed, especially when backing out of parking lots. Remember as we discussed in the Backing Accident module, do not over-back! Remember, back up just enough to get you out safely.

DIA Focus Concepts in Parking Lots:

Maintain a safe speed at all times.
Continual visual scanning
Proper horn usage—communicate!
Avoid over-backing in parking lots!

The Two Most Frequent Accidents:
Backing and Parking Lots (3)

Parking Lots

Why is it a frequent accident?

- High number of vehicles in motion in congested area
- **Blind spots galore!**
- High-speed drivers in parking lots
- **Visibility at times reduced**
- Vehicles backing out

The Two Most Frequent Accidents: Backing and Parking Lots (4)

Focus Concepts:

- **DETECT AND EXPECT**—scan area for backup lights and blind spots.
- **COMMUNICATE** with proper horn usage—BEEP-BEEP
- **MAINTAIN SLOW, SAFE SPEED** in parking lots

Minor damage accidents but still costly —$$$

Blind-Side Pullouts

If this applies to you, it is a very important habit that you need to eliminate. Avoid parking on the street with your vehicle facing in the wrong direction. Here are some photos of vehicles parked in this manner.

When you pull out, you are pulling out on your blind side, and this can be dangerous.

Also, if another vehicle hits your vehicle, since you were parked facing the wrong way, you may not have a claim against the other party. Simply put, eliminate parking incorrectly!

Avoid incorrect parking to eliminate Blindside pullouts!

Proper Horn Usage

If I were getting ready to drive somewhere and while doing my pre-drive vehicle inspection, I find out my horn is not working, I would not drive the vehicle! It is that important! I would go to nearest auto repair center immediately. The horn is your communicator to others when they decide to pull out in front of you, or another unsafe maneuver. The horn is free, and the results of not using it properly can be expensive! When you detect a vehicle at an intersection and you see the wheels start rolling, tapping your horn is essential. You are alerting the other driver that you are approaching. They may not have seen you or in a hurry to pull out; by communicating, you are helping them make the decision to wait.

Not tapping horn and having to blast your horn may be too late, and the next sound could be a CRASH! If you find yourself blasting your horn a lot, it may be that you are driving too aggressively or you are not being a good detector during your driving missions.

When it comes to pedestrians, bicyclists, and motorcyclists, you need to tap horn at a proper time when that situation arises. Tapping your horn at a bicyclist when you are too close may scare them, and they may turn their head and drift toward you! If you tap the horn too far away, they may not even hear the horn. Only tap the horn if needed based on each situation; be proactive.

Horn usage is very important in parking lots. Anytime I back up in my driveway or in a parking lot, I immediately tap my horn a couple of times. This is after I physically check the rear of the vehicle. Communicating to others with your horn is so important because of blind spots and people driving too fast in the parking lots. By scanning and communicating, you should prevent any possible accidents in these parking lots.

The Focus Concept: YOUR HORN IS FREE. NOT USING IT CAN BE EXPENSIVE! AND TAPPING IT WILL PREVENT BLASTING IT!

Proper Horn Usage

- Horn usage communication on the road is very important.
- If your horn is not working, do not drive!
- IF YOU ARE BLASTING HORN TOO MUCH = AGGRESSIVE DRIVER AND A POOR DETECTOR!
- PROPER TIMING IN COMMUNICATING with bicyclists, pedestrians, and motorcyclists is critically important!
- When backing, tapping the horn must be an automatic disciplined habit!

➢ **SCENARIO**:

    You Detect a vehicle at parking lot exit. Your next step is to Expect the vehicle to either move or stay still.
  - ✓ If the vehicle's wheels move, tap your horn communicating to the other driver and help them make the decision to stay.

➢ **FOCUS CONCEPT**:

    The horn is free to use. Not using it can be expensive or deadly. Tapping eliminates blasting!

Minus 5, Minus 10

I preach "Minus 5, Minus 10 MPH" anytime you are driving at night, in low and narrow visibility areas, and during inclement weather (rain, snow, and ice).

Analyze your area and see in what areas you need to reduce your speed (again, according to visibility). Areas with a lot of hills and curves and heavily wooded areas fall into this category also.

When driving at night in these areas, you need to remember "Minus 5, Minus 10 MPH"! And remember, many serious hydroplaning accidents can be prevented by applying the "Minus 5, Minus 10" focus concept, especially when it is raining at night. I have driven when the rain is very heavy and blinding. I reduce my speed according to these conditions and immediately put my emergency flashers on to alert traffic behind me. If necessary, I would pull into a safe place off the road completely until the storm passes. Don't take chances!

Focus Concept: DRIVING IN RAINY, INCLEMENT WEATHER AND IN LOW AND NARROW VISIBILITY AREAS WHEN DRIVING AT NIGHT = MINUS 5, MINUS 10 MPH MINIMUM.

Hydroplaning is the result when the driver does not adjust speed according to inclement weather conditions.

Remember the "Minus 5, Minus 10 MPH" focus concept!

Interstate and Rural Highway Driving

When I am driving these high-speed expressways and tolls, this is like major league! I must be 100 percent focused and in control of what is going on all around me. It's no secret that accidents on interstate and rural highways usually result in very serious or fatal results. When I drive on these roads, I see many drivers flying by me, even as I am going the posted speed limit in either lane! You have seen them, I am sure; they weave in and out and make abrupt lane changes without signaling! If this is you, please understand you need to change before you become a statistic, or involve others and they become a statistic! If you make a hundred lane changes, you need to signal a hundred times, simple as that!

On many occasions, the primary person causing the accident survives and impacts their fellow drivers much more.

The focus concepts are primarily as follows:

Be well rested—lost control, rollovers, and striking fixed objects are the types of accidents resulting from dozing off at the wheel! It is said that driving when not well rested is much more dangerous than being under the influence.

Eliminate distractions, improper steering habits, and unsafe speeds. Drive according to the available visibility and weather conditions.

<u>Preplan and signal your lane changes 100 percent of the time!</u> Extremely important!

On two-lane rural highways and four-lane undivided, ensure you follow proper passing procedures.

Check your mirrors on a consistent basis for traffic behind you or passing you. It is very important for preplanning all your lane changes.

<u>STAY AWAY FROM THE GROUPIES!</u> Avoid being too close to the other cars that are bunched up traveling on these higher-speed highways.

And remember THE CONTINUAL-CRUISING EGGSHELL! Don't crack the eggshell!

Have a Strategic lane Driving Plan, especially on your regular routes, such as to work/store/ church.

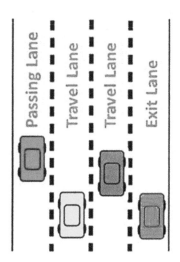

- • **Know your LANE MERGES!**
- • <u>Preplan</u> your lane changes.
- • Avoid **abrupt** lane changes.
- • **Minimize** lane changes.
- ➢ <u>**Focus Concepts:**</u> Detect and expect, and **<u>blend in</u>**.

Warning Signs—Our Guides to a Safe Trip

Every time you get behind the wheel, you want to be a Warning Sign Scanner. There are various types of warning signs, such as low-visibility areas, sharp curves, lane mergers, and lane directions, to name a few.

As a DIA-Certified Teen Driver, you must make it a disciplined habit to scan and process what each sign is guiding you to do or be aware of.

Speed limit signs are simple to understand. These speed limits are when the roads are dry and in safe condition. Once there is rain, snow, or loose gravel, you know you must reduce your speed according to these conditions.

Look closely for lane merge signs (for example, where three lanes merge into two lanes), especially in the areas you frequent. These areas I classify as DangerZones because of drivers not being aware, and you could end up being cut off.

Work Construction Zones—Be prepared to reduce your speed, and watch for workers or road construction equipment moving around the area Also, fines in work construction zones are usually doubled!

Signs warning "low visibility" automatically demand a reduced speed. Warning signs are a communicator and the guide to making your drive safer.

DIA Focus Concept:

Be a warning sign scanner.

This is an extremely important habit to execute on all your driving missions.

WARNING SIGNS—your guides for a safe trip!

- Be a **warning sign scanner**!
- Obeying speed limit signs = $$$ savings! <u>Remember the 1520 rule</u>.
- Lane merger signs
- Construction warning signs
- Low-visibility signs

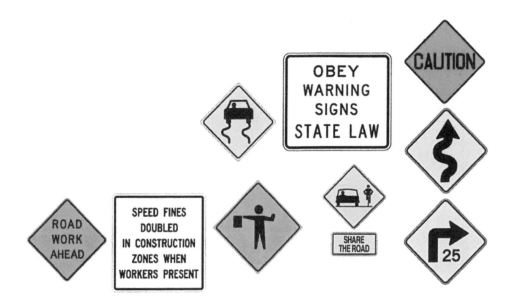

Understanding "The Seven Pitfalls of Teen Drivers"

1. **A Complacent Attitude**—Most teens have the attitude of invulnerability; the "nothing can happen to me" attitude, or "I know it already," is alive and well. After the initial defensive-driver training, the attitude of not needing to follow all the habits learned can develop. After a couple of months, the initial habits learned in Drivers Ed become less important, and teens become lax. Remember, this first phase of the teen driver is extremely critical, and the accident risks are extremely high. They need to **avoid the danger word—complacency**! The first two habits that change soon after initial training are the ability to maintain a safe speed at all times (adjusting speed according to available visibility) and not avoiding distractions!

Webster's defines complacency as being "self-satisfied and content with one's own ability." Complacent drivers, especially beginners, place themselves in a very vulnerable position. Remember, everyone is vulnerable on the public highways.

The Teen Driver's Bible is designed to concentrate on focus concepts and keep the training simple. We will repeat the need to eliminate the two main root causes of accidents—DISTRACTIONS AND SPEEDING—over and over for retention purposes.

And the simple solutions of following the "1520 rule (the solution to eliminate speeding!" and completing DIA's Pre-Drive Check and Setup Routine (the solution which helps eliminate distractions!) will be highlighted, and of course, **NEVER EVER TEXTING WHILE THE WHEELS ARE ROLLING!**

We want to prevent the teen driver from being an offensive/aggressive driver, instead becoming a 100 percent focused and in-control teen driver from point A to point B! A teen driver running late is a recipe for possible serious accidents!

2. **Not maintaining proper speed control at all <u>times</u>!**

This is primarily caused by several reasons or situations. The main reason is not planning or not leaving in sufficient time to reach your destination in a timely manner. This automatically makes the new teen driver an offensive/aggressive driver who is primarily concerned with arriving at his or her destination on time. When running late, disciplined good driving habits are quickly forgotten, along with the ability to focus on proper defensive-driving habits. This is an extremely huge cause of many accidents involving new teen drivers. Hastiness and rash decisions can take over quickly!

Another critical situation occurs with the changes in weather such as rain, snow, fog, and excessive winds with your teen running late. The time in which highways become the most dangerous is at the beginning of a rainstorm, when the water mixes with the oil already on the roads. This can turn the surface into a glasslike condition. The most important focus concept for the teen driver is reducing speed according to conditions and increasing following distance when following vehicles ahead. Follow the Continual-Cruising Eggshell focus concept (refer to the Continual-Cruising Eggshell module). The first conclusion when investigating an accident where the weather changed drastically is the teen driver was driving too fast for conditions! DIA's focus concept for these weather conditions is Minus 5, Minus 10 MPH. The focus is to avoid losing control and hydroplaning, which means to reduce speed 5–10 mph, or more if needed. Add hills and curves, and this can make drive extremely dangerous! Again, the focus concept to eliminate any speeding on your driving mission is to be a disciplined 1520 driver.

3. **Poor visibility/detection habits**—The eye habits of teen drivers have not developed properly, and one of DIA's learning techniques is to establish fundamental eye habits which will teach you where to look as you drive, as you start up, as you slow down, and as you encounter different highway or road situations. By focusing on these low-visibility areas, you learn to become a driver who detects and expects a possible accident situation ahead of time. These eye habits will be explained further in this book and in the diagrams. Focus concept: when your visibility is reduced, creating a possible DangerZone, you simply reduce your speed! Detect and expect, be an active scanner, and be proactive vs. reactive! Refer to DIA's 12 DangerZones module.

Lack of steering control—Driving with only one hand on the wheel is the result of several situations, such as playing with the radio/CD/MP3 player, drinking while driving, smoking while driving, using cell phone to talk or text, map-reading, eating, combing hair, applying makeup, or several of these done at the same time! Also, looking down for articles or looking while talking with your passenger while the wheels are rolling is trouble! You need to be proactive and in control, as if you were to have a blowout all of a sudden while driving on a curve!

Focus concept: When the wheels are rolling, you can't be looking down, texting, or looking at passengers! Many lost-control type of accidents involving teen drivers are caused by the above poor habits as well as driving too fast around curves. These accidents are extremely dangerous, with serious consequences. Remember, lost-control type of accidents have become the #1 teen killer on the roads today. Proper steering at all times is a must!

4. **In-vehicle distractions**—Similar to pitfall #3, this is a real biggie. This has been a cause of many accidents involving teen drivers. This is where the teen needs to learn the discipline of keeping their eyes on the road always and avoid being distracted when the wheels are rolling. DIA's solution: DIA instructs the teen driver, along with the parent/guardian with the PRE-DRIVE CHECK AND SETUP ROUTINE. See module.

Also, parents, when you are in the passenger seat and your teen is driving, make sure when they are talking to you, they do not look at you when the wheels are rolling! Teach them to continue to look forward, focusing on the road ahead as they are talking without having to look at you—very important during initial training.

Last but most critical is proper adjustment of the mirrors. These are to be adjusted in a manner to ensure maximum visibility (minimizing your blind spots). The proper adjustment of your mirrors is extremely critical to a safe trip. See diagrams.

5. **Unfamiliar area and improper trip planning**—Not knowing the specifics of the final destination greatly can become a visual distraction (unfamiliarity, scenery, other drivers, and billboards) Refer to your GPS or map prior to departing, know the numbering system and major hundred blocks of cross intersections. Also, what side of the street is your destination at? Is it an even or odd address? By knowing the hundred blocks of the major cross street intersections and the even/odd numbering system, you can focus more on the road ahead.

Example: You are going to 5604 Broadway. Your GPS or map shows Lake Creek, which is a major cross street as 5500 block; therefore, 5604 will be one block after you pass Lake Creek. Note: It is extremely crucial that you plan and review all new trips with your teen driver. It is important the new teen driver is not referring to GPS or map while the wheels are rolling. Have a complete strategic lane driving plan for all your regular driving missions, and remember to know all your lane endings. Refer to "Your Teen's First Year Driving Plan" module.

6. **High anxiety, hastiness, and the HD factor.** Instead of driving safely, concentrating on disciplined defensive-driving habits, proper speed control, and staying in control until reaching their destination all go out the window because of the high anxiety, excitement about driving, and hastiness of the teen driver. The solution is to start a regimented routine of slowing down your lifestyle and habits. Avoid being hasty and in a hurry. Again, plan ahead accordingly and avoid becoming an inexperienced, aggressive driver!

The HD FACTOR is what I call anyone who becomes the HOTDOG driver. This person needs to be advised immediately by his or her friends that they are driving too fast. The headlines have told us the story of the teenagers who were killed because a young teen driver was showing off and driving too fast! There was an accident where two drivers started racing and one broadsided a turning vehicle, resulting in several fatalities!

I tell parents to take a close look at their teen and analyze them. Are they laid back? Hyper? Always running late? Those who are consistently hyper or running late—this is a huge red flag that needs to be addressed immediately! I strongly suggest they discuss making the 1520 rule as PRIORITY 1 every time they have a driving mission. If there is a tendency to show off in front of their friends, this is another sign that needs to be addressed immediately! Hopefully, they are not driving a high-performance vehicle. Also, discuss that they should never exceed the posted speed limits when they are on a driving mission. Our mission is focused on prevention and your survival!

7. **Peer pressure/drinking/drugs**—Peer pressure with drinking and driving is a pitfall that has caused countless senseless tragedies. In this first phase of driving, you cannot afford to give in to peer pressure. Drinking while driving results in many negative consequences. DUI's citations run in the thousands of dollars when it is all over. Fatalities and serious injuries can easily occur when driving impaired!

As a new DIA-Certified Teen Driver, you must understand you are responsible for yourself, your family, and your community to always drive in a safe manner. You must understand this when someone says, "Let's see how fast you can drive this car."

Never ever let peer pressure override your responsibility! It can quickly change your life and your privilege to drive! The statistics speak for themselves; **DRINKING AND DRIVING DO NOT MIX! YOU CANNOT DO BOTH! IT'S THAT SIMPLE!** (See Alcohol-Related Statistics.)

I, _____, have received a copy of "Understanding the Seven Pitfalls of Teen Drivers." I understand them and will concentrate on eliminating all of these pitfalls. I understand that driving is a privilege and can be taken away. I will focus 100 percent on my driving every time I get behind the wheel.

_____

Signature   Date

_____

Printed Name

The Ten Commandments of the DIA-Certified Teen Driver

1. I will be a **DISCIPLINED 1520 driver** by departing in sufficient time that I arrive at my destination a minimum of 15–20 minutes ahead of schedule. This will eliminate any need to speed, will **avoid hasty pullouts** at intersections, and give me time to compensate for other drivers. I understand a teen driver running late is a recipe for very serious consequences! Initials _____

2. I will complete a proper Pre-Drive Vehicle Condition Inspection to ensure all signal lights, backup lights, brakes, mirrors, and tires in proper operational condition. Initials_____

3. **I will complete a thorough DIA <u>Pre-Drive Check and Setup Routine</u>** by adjusting my mirrors for maximum rear field of vision (<u>and using all three mirrors together</u>), following DIA proper mirror adjustment focus concept. I will set radio/CD/MP3 player prior to departure and secure all items and eliminate any possible distractions while the wheels are rolling. I will also eliminate distraction from passengers speaking to me, by focusing on the road and not looking at them while the wheels are rolling. I will eliminate any texting while the wheels are rolling. Initials_____

4. I will fasten my seat belt without fail prior to starting the vehicle. When backing up, I will physically check the rear prior to backing up, tap horn, and avoid over-backing! Initials_____

5. I will be a 100-percenter, by signaling 100 percent of the time when changing lanes or making turns. I will PREPLAN all my lane changes 100 percent of the time and avoid any abrupt lane changes 100 percent of the time. Initials_____

6. I will have a strategic lane driving plan for all my regular routes, minimize as many left turns, attempt to make them in controlled intersections, and I will know all the lane endings and lane merges of these regular routes. Initials_____

7. I will eliminate any blind-spot driving and be staggered/offset when needed (leaving an opening always, especially to the right). I will be proactive versus reactive. Initials_____

8. I will be focused on detecting and expecting any possible conflicts due to reduced visibility (hills, curves, buildings, and trees causing blind spots) and reduce my speed accordingly. Also, I will detect and expect vehicles when approaching on ramps and off-ramps, and be prepared for any abrupt lane changes, or being cut off by them. I understand the focus concept of blending in in these on-ramp and off-ramp areas. Initials_____

9. I will observe and comply with all speed limit and warning signs, and reduce speed (**Minus 5, Minus 10 MPH**) accordingly, especially during inclement weather and night driving missions. Initials_____

10. Understanding my responsibility to myself, my family, and my community, I will avoid any peer pressure to drive at unsafe speeds and be **100 PERCENT FOCUSED AND IN CONTROL FROM POINT A to POINT B**. I will avoid driving if not well rested, or under the influence. Initials_____

Signature:_____ Date Reviewed:_____

Driving Institute of America's curriculum is focused on preventative fundamental-focus concepts and not liable for action or inaction of anyone who is driving in various situations. DIA does not guarantee you will never be in an accident since approximately 10 percent of all accidents are not preventable. As a person behind the wheel, you have a goal to follow all preventative measures that will help prevent any accident from occurring.

DIA-Certified Teen Driver Certification and Pledge

Eliminate complacent attitude

1. As a DIA-Certified Teen Driver, I understand my mission is to survive the critical first phase of driving. I know the risks for 17- to 19-year-old teens are four times higher to be in a serious accident, and at 16 years, my risks are eight times higher! I understand that I am most vulnerable at this period of my life, and I know I must be disciplined in executing all the focus concepts taught in this curriculum. I pledge to make all what I have learned disciplined habits and follow the plan of being 100 percent focused and In Control from Point A to Point B on every single driving mission.

   _____ DIA-Certified Teen Driver Signature

2. As a DIA-Certified Teen Driver, I understand not to have a complacent attitude and understand that I am responsible for my well-being, my family, and my community at all times and that it is a privilege to drive. I also understand my life can change in a split second as I enter the most dangerous place in the world—the public highways. Therefore, the DIA focus concepts and fundamental habits are what I will follow always.

   _____ DIA-Certified Teen Driver Signature

As the parent/guardian of my DIA-Certified Teen Driver, I pledge to spend sufficient time with my teen and set the example by following all the DIA focus concepts myself and DangerZone Roadtests (TM pending). I will follow "Your teen driver's first-year driving plan" and analyze all the DangerZones of each route, and if any alternate routes, we will decide which is the safest route to drive. I will look at the DIA training timeline (which focuses on not allowing our 16-year-old to drive, but recommend start at age 17). If I allow my teen to drive before 17, I will still drive the first five routes for six months with my teen, then my teen may drive when I feel teen is ready. A commentary is completed on every route driven by me and my teen.

   _____ Parent/Guardian Signature

Maintain a safe speed

3. As a DIA-Certified Teen Driver, I understand that maintaining a safe speed is critical and that speeding is one of the two major root causes of accidents, along with distractions, **I understand the 1520 rule is the #1 focus concept to eliminate speeding altogether, and I pledge to be a disciplined 1520 driver by departing every time with the plan of arriving at my destination 15–20 minutes ahead of schedule. I will not be an offensive, aggressive driver!**

   I know I must live by the 1520 rule; it is that important! I also pledge to eliminate any hasty pullouts at intersections and compensate for other drivers who may be speeding.

   As a DIA-Certified Teen Driver, I understand the focus concept "when visibility is reduced (blind spots, buildings. curves and hills), I will simply reduce my speed," and I pledge to do this always.

   Also, I will reduce speed immediately during adverse weather conditions, and night driving (especially when it first starts to rain, sleet, snow, and windy conditions). **I understand this: rain + hills or curves + excessive speed = possible disaster!** So, I pledge to execute the focus concept of Minus 5, Minus 10 MPH (minimum) during these situations.

   _____

   DIA-Certified Teen Driver Signature

Eliminate all distractions

4. As a DIA-Certified Teen Driver, I understand that distractions are the second major root cause of vehicle accidents. I understand DIA's Pre-Drive Check and Setup Routine is the main solution for eliminating all in-vehicle distractions (eliminating texting) while the wheels are rolling. I pledge to be organized by securing all items in my vehicle and set up radio/CD/MP3 player **prior** to departure. When a passenger is in the front seat, I pledge to avoid looking at them if we are talking while the wheels are rolling, instead focus on the road. I also will adjust mirrors the DIA way: adjust out to minimize blind spots on both sides of vehicle and **always using in conjunction with the middle mirror**. I pledge to be 100 percent in control and detecting and expecting any accident possibilities during my driving mission.

   _____

   DIA-Certified Teen Driver Signature

   As the parent/guardian of the DIA-Certified Teen Driver, I pledge to ensure the vehicle is properly equipped and safe to drive at all times and that it **is not** to be driven if horn or mirrors are not in proper working condition

   _____

   Parent/Guardian Signature

Be a 100 percent In Control DIA-Certified Teen Driver

5. As a DIA-Certified Teen Driver I understand that the lost-control type of accident is the #1 most deadly type of accident involving teen drivers. I understand the importance of proper control of

the steering wheel at all times, and I pledge to be prepared by having hands in proper 10-2 position consistently in the event of a blowout (especially on curves). I pledge to be proactive and stay in control at all times when driving.

As a DIA-Certified Teen Driver, I understand the focus concept "When the wheels are rolling, I can't be looking down, texting, or looking at any passengers." I also pledge to avoid playing with radio/CD/MP3 player or looking for articles while the wheels are rolling.

DIA-Certified Teen Driver Signature

Have a strategic lane driving plan and know all lane endings and merges

6. As a DIA-Certified Teen Driver, I understand the focus concept of having a strategic lane driving plan, for my regular driving missions. I pledge that when I make the decision to be in the left lane, I will attempt to BE STAGGERED/OFFSET as much as possible, to create an opening into the right lane. I pledge to be proactive versus reactive should the oncoming traffic cross the centerline! I pledge to be disciplined in all the lane strategies covered in the Strategic Lane Driving Plan module. I also pledge to know all the lane endings at all major intersections and lane merges, especially on all my regular driving missions. I understand the problems that arise when making left turns, and I will choose to go to controlled intersections whenever possible if needing to make left turns.

DIA-Certified Teen Driver Signature

Approach all intersections with caution and eliminate rolling stops

7. As a DIA-Certified Teen Driver, I understand that a green light does not mean go, but instead "go—proceeding with caution." I pledge to be prepared in the event of the cross traffic not stopping when they have a red light, or when approaching blind intersections. I also pledge to eliminate any rolling stops or hasty pullouts and to judge the speed of cross traffic before pulling out. Again, being disciplined in the 1520 rule will help me avoid being offensive and will allow for safe pullouts at every intersection. I pledge to reduce speed at any blind intersections. In residential intersections where I do not have a stop sign, I will clear each intersection according to available visibility.

DIA-Certified Teen Driver Signature

Lack of experience

8. As a DIA-Certified Teen Driver, I understand my lack of experience is a huge drawback, and my eye habits are not completely developed as to knowing all the DangerZones. I pledge to reduce my speed when approaching hills and curves because of my visibility being reduced. Again, I pledge to eliminate the two main root causes of accidents with teens, distractions and speeding when I drive.

DIA-Certified Teen Driver Signature

Peer pressure

9. As a DIA-Certified Teen Driver, I understand I must be mature enough to avoid taking any risks when behind the wheel. I pledge never to be influenced by my peers in any way to drive my vehicle in an unsafe manner. I understand when someone says, "Let's see how fast we can go," this can lead to a very dangerous situation. I pledge to be responsible for my well-being, my family, my friends, and my community always when behind the wheel.

_____   DIA-Certified Teen Driver Signature

Drinking and driving

10. As a DIA-Certified Teen Driver, I understand that drinking and driving may lead to a much higher possibility of a serious accident! I pledge, during this critical first phase of driving, never to get behind the wheel under the influence. I pledge to avoid taking any risks while getting behind the wheel, and my goal is to survive the 16- to 19-year-old driver's critical first phase of driving. I pledge to be a responsible teen driver protecting myself, and all the occupants in my vehicle.

_____   DIA-Certified Teen Driver Signature

Protecting my space

11. As a DIA-Certified Teen Driver, I understand the focus concept of protecting my space and the focus concept of staying away from the Groupies on high-speed highways.
    I pledge to always protect my space by controlling the traffic behind me. I will execute the Continual- Cruising Eggshell focus concept to protect my front space and vehicle at all times. This focus concept will help you eliminate making abrupt stops.

_____   DIA-Certified Teen Driver Signature

The DIA-Certified Teen Driver vs. the Teen Driver

12. As a DIA-Certified Teen Driver, I understand the difference in a teen driver versus the DIA-Certified Teen Driver based on the DIA curriculum. I pledge to learn all the FOCUS CONCEPTS and the nineteen DIA-Certified Teen Driver elements and to be disciplined to make them routine habits. My goal is to follow all the DIA-Certified Teen Driver focus concepts throughout my life.

_____   DIA- Certified Teen Driver Signature

BEING A DIA TEEN 100-PERCENTER RECAP

13. I pledge to be a DIA TEEN 100-percenter when it comes to the following:

- I will be a disciplined 1520 driver 100 percent of the time by planning to arrive at my destination 15–20 minutes ahead of time. I know it will make all my driving missions less stressful. This is the solution that eliminates speed and hasty decisions.
- I will not have a complacent attitude and will plan my driving mission 100 percent of the time.
- I will complete a thorough Pre-Drive Check and Setup Routine every time I get behind the wheel. This is the solution to eliminate any possible distractions!
- I will not text or answer the phone while the wheels are rolling. I will drive to a safe area 100 percent of the time for phone calls or texting needs.
- I will not look at any passengers while the wheels are rolling, 100 percent of the time.
- I will adjust my mirrors the DIA way for optimal rear vision 100 percent of the time and use all three mirrors together.
- I will fasten my seatbelt 100 percent of the time.
- I will eliminate any rolling stops and hasty pullouts at intersections 100 percent of the time.
- I will physically check the rear of my vehicle every time before I back up 100 percent.
- I will tap my horn prior to backing up 100 percent of the time.
- I will avoid over-backing 100 percent of the time.
- I will SIGNAL and PREPLAN all lane changes and turns 100 percent of the time.
- I will eliminate making any ABRUPT lane changes 100 percent of the time.
- I will go to the next crossroad to make a safer turn versus making U-turn from shoulder.
- I will plan on being STAGGERED/OFFSET, and having an opening whenever possible, especially when driving in the left lane (being proactive vs. reactive 100 percent of the time).
- I will focus on knowing all the lane endings on my regular routes 100 percent of the time.
- I will drive all my routes with the plan of minimizing left turns 100 percent of the time.
- When stopped in traffic, preparing to make a left turn, I WILL NOT have wheels turned until making the turn 100 percent of the time.
- I will try to go to controlled intersections vs. uncontrolled intersections when having to make left turns, whenever possible.
- I will have a strategic lane driving plan for all my regular driving missions 100 percent of the time, and with the goal of minimizing lane changes.
- I will be proactive versus reactive by proper horn usage 100 percent of the time.
- I will reduce speed when approaching hills and curves (due to reduced visibility) 100 percent of the time.
- I will focus on all warning signs, and be aware of bicyclists, motorcyclists, and pedestrians 100 percent of the time.
- I will execute DIA's In-and-Out Night Vision focus concept 100 percent of the time when pulling out, or turning at all intersections at night.
- I will activate my night vision when driving at night 100 percent of the time.
- I will protect my space by controlling the traffic behind me 100 percent of the time.
- I will eliminate any tailgating and stay away from the GROUPIES 100 percent of the time.

- I will execute the Continual-Cruising Eggshell focus concept, and not crack the eggshell 100 percent of the time.
- I will reduce my speed a minimum of Minus 5, Minus 10 MPH (from posted speed limit) when driving in bad weather (avoiding possible hydroplaning), and at night because of poor visibility.
- I will drive at safe speeds in residential areas and being constantly aware of children in front of parked vehicles (looking for feet!) 100 percent of the time.
- I will avoid following vehicles with heavy machinery, landscaping, and open trailers with various loose items whenever possible.
- I will make sure of being well-rested prior to any long trips 100 percent of the time.
- I will avoid driving in the left lane at night when going over an overpass, or curve when on divided highways, 100 percent of the time, knowing there could be a possible WRONG-WAY DRIVER!
- I will not give in to peer pressure of driving faster than posted speed limits 100 percent of the time.
- I will not drive at any time while under the influence of alcohol. I understand this is a huge risk for possible serious accidents!
- I will be focused and 100 percent In Control from Point A to Point B 100 percent of the time.

The DIA-Certified Teen Driver Certification and Pledge and DIA 100-Percenter Sign-Off

I, _____, understand I am responsible for my well-being, to my family, and my community to drive in a responsible manner every time I get behind the wheel. I commit to being a disciplined DIA-Certified Teen Driver by following all the focus concepts and training in this curriculum. I have reviewed all the diagrams in DIA's curriculum and understand them completely, and I plan on executing the focus-concept habits taught.

_____

Signature   Printed Name   Date

Driving Institute's curriculum is focused on preventative safety concepts and is not liable for any action or inaction of anyone who is driving under various situations. Every trainee's goal when driving behind the wheel is to follow all the preventative measures taught and to be proactive versus reactive.

The DIA-Certified Teen Driver Certification and Pledge, copyright 2013, is property of Driving Institute of America and may not be reproduced without the express written consent of Driving Institute of America.

The DIA-Certified Teen Driver vs. the Teen Driver

My philosophy is very simple: driving is like painting a picture or completing a puzzle. It's a long process until it is finally finished. Again, the most dangerous word when it comes to driving and people's attitude toward driving is COMPLACENCY. As I explained in the introduction of this book and videos, almost every driver would say, "I'm a good driver." It is very difficult to get any driver to go through a defensive-driving course, and they need to learn just how quickly they may be killed because of very simple errors in judgment or bad habits. This module is a summary of what I have learned in thirty-nine years in the transportation field. If you **follow what the DIA-Certified Teen Driver does and** avoid **what the regular teen driver does, this will help you during your first phase of driving and hopefully forever!**

I have been driving over fifty years. Eleven and a half of those years, I drove approximately 1,000 miles each week in the transportation field. As we discussed earlier, each time you go to the store, then the library, then cleaners would be a total of four missions (mission 1 is going to store, mission 2 from store to library, mission 3 is library to cleaners, mission 4 is cleaners then returning home).

In my 11.5 years of driving, I averaged 77 missions (delivery or p/u stops) per day × 22 days per month × 12 months × 11.5 years, which equals 233,772 missions. The total miles during this equaled approximately 572,760 miles; these were only at-work miles. I am still continually driving with an attitude of "I must be 100 percent focused and in control from point A to point B for each and every mission." I am not a paranoid driver, but instead, I'm a "staying in control until reaching my destination" type of driver. My mission is to be detecting and expecting throughout, and being proactive versus reactive.

Now, below I will describe what DIA considers a DIA-Certified Teen Driver vs. the teen driver. There is a huge difference! This is my recipe, if you will, for improving your knowledge, behavior, and driving skills.

Remember this: focused discipline is the key, along with continued practice, and understanding of all the focus concepts you will need to make habits.

The one time you fail to follow the 1520 rule may be the time you become involved in a serious accident. Knowing that you are running behind, you suddenly become an aggressive driver! Remember this. You must immediately say to yourself, "I'm not going to go back to my old habits. If I am late, so be it. I will drive with 100 percent focus, maintain a safe speed, eliminate being hasty, and stay in control." Instead, pull over to a safe area and call someone letting them know you will be a little late.

Offensive drivers eventually become statistics! Remember, aggressive/offensive drivers become less defensive drivers as they reduce their reaction time when conflicts arise!

Now, let us get to the last module, "The DIA-Certified Teen Driver vs. the Teen Driver." Safe driving!

PROPER KNOWLEDGE + FOCUSED DISCIPLINED HABITS = ACCIDENT PREVENTION!

The DIA-Certified Teen Driver vs. the Teen Driver™

The DIA Certified Teen Driver understands their mission of being 100 percent focused and in control from point A to point B, is well rested, and understands the two main root causes of accidents are distractions and speeding and focuses on always eliminating them.

The teen driver is easily distracted and does not control speed consistently according to changing visibility or conditions. The teen driver at times drives when fatigued.

The DIA Certified Teen Driver knows the condition of the vehicle; regarding tires, brakes, signal lights, backup lights/brake lights, horn, and wipers. The DIA Certified Teen Driver adjusts mirrors properly for maximum rear visibility and minimizes blind-spot areas and uses all three mirrors together when checking rear.

The teen driver rarely checks or looks at these items. The teen driver does not have mirrors adjusted properly and blind spots are much bigger.

The DIA Certified Teen Driver understands, is disciplined, and lives by the 1520 rule, understanding that planning on arriving 15–20 minutes ahead of schedule creates a less stressful drive, helps compensate for other drivers, and eliminates the need for speed! The DIA Certified Teen Driver is almost always at the destination a minimum of 15–20 minutes prior to appointment time. This is now a disciplined habit.

The teen driver departs late at times and is very aggressive throughout the drive. Speeding, making hasty pullouts at intersections, making erratic and abrupt lane changes, failing to signal, tailgating, missing exit ramps, and running red lights are typical for this driver. This driver eventually may become a statistic. The lost-control/rollover accident, striking fixed object, and intersection accidents are high possibilities!

The DIA-Certified Teen Driver is a 100-Percenter and fastens seat belt 100 percent of the time prior to the vehicle being in motion.

The teen driver is not a 100-percenter fastening seat belt.

The DIA-Certified Teen Driver completes the DIA Pre-Drive Check and Setup Routine, eliminating all in-vehicle distractions and is organized. The DIA-Certified Teen Driver knows you can't be looking down, texting, or looking at any passengers when the wheels are rolling!

The teen driver is not aware of all the in-vehicle distractions and does not have a pre-drive check and setup routine; therefore, in-vehicle distractions are a high possibility. Unorganized, the teen driver looks down a lot, texts, and looks at passengers while the wheels are rolling!

The DIA-Certified Teen Driver understands each driving mission and tries to drive routes with minimal left turns (especially with uncontrolled intersections). The DIA-Certified Teen Driver protects space by controlling vehicles coming from behind when approaching lights, stop signs, or when making left turns. The DIA-Certified Teen Driver understands the focus concept that being rear-ended by another vehicle can be prevented.

The DIA-Certified Teen Driver vs. the Teen Driver™

The teen driver is not aware of problems left turns may cause or how to prevent being rear-ended by another vehicle and does not protect space in front of vehicle consistently.

The DIA-Certified Teen Driver is a 100-Percenter and <u>signals</u> 100 percent of the time when making lane changes and turns.

The teen driver is <u>not consistent and lazy</u> when it comes to signaling lane changes or turns. This teen driver is not a 100-percenter!

<u>The DIA-Certified Teen Driver has a strategic lane driving plan</u>, pre-plans all lane changes, and minimizes the number of lane changes on a given driving route. The DIA Certified Teen Driver does not make abrupt lane changes.

The teen driver does not preplan lane changes, and lane changes can be abrupt. The teen driver does not have a strategic lane driving plan.

The DIA-Certified Teen Driver is proactive when using the horn, by being a good detector. The DIA-Certified Teen Driver is proactive in communicating to other drivers. This helps alert other drivers to make the decision to stay. The goal is to eliminate any horn blasts, and skids! The DIA-Certified Teen Driver does not take any chances and <u>knows the horn is free and not using it can be expensive!</u>

The teen driver usually blasts their horn, or skids because of being late in detecting or being aggressive, and not expecting conflicts! Usually after the horn blast, you may hear a crash! Being reactive is simply too late!

The DIA-Certified Teen Driver has consistent proper steering habits (hands at 10 and 2) and maintains good control throughout driving mission. This disciplined habit is especially important on curves and downhill roads. This avoids a possible rollover or losing control in the event of a blowout!

The teen driver's steering habits are erratic and inconsistent. In the event of a blowout, losing control or rolling the vehicle over is a high possibility! The teen driver sometimes only uses one hand.

The DIA-Certified Teen Driver maintains a safe proper speed in all types of conditions. Adjusts speed during inclement weather and low visibility areas. The DIA-Certified Teen Driver <u>understands when approaching curves and hills, visibility is reduced, and reduces speed accordingly</u> by using focus concept Minus 5, Minus 10 MPH.

The teen driver is not always aware of speed and is at the mercy of possibly running late. This teen driver is at times offensive and not aware of reducing speed when approaching curves and hills. The teen driver does not adjust speed according to inclement weather (hydroplaning possibilities are higher).

The DIA-Certified Teen Driver vs. the Teen Driver™

The DIA-Certified Teen Driver understands lane strategies and is prepared for conflicts. The DIA-Certified Teen Driver <u>understands being staggered/offset as much as possible and not being boxed in is safer</u>. He/she tries to have an opening to a safer lane as needed, and <u>minimizes driving in someone's blind spot</u>. The DIA-Certified Teen Driver does not attempt to pass in left lane when oncoming traffic is coming <u>whenever possible</u>, especially on undivided highways. The DIA-Certified Teen Driver is knowledgeable of all lane endings and lane merges, especially on all local and regular routes.

The teen driver is not aware of lane strategies. The teen driver drives in the other driver's blind spot and usually gets boxed in. This driver does not know or concentrate on lane endings or merges and cuts others off at exit/entrance ramps. The teen driver makes abrupt lane changes.

The DIA-Certified Teen Driver <u>detects and expects ahead of time when approaching on-ramps and off-ramps</u>. He/she knows the focus concept of <u>blending in</u> properly, makes adjustments, and is prepared for the other driver's abrupt lane changes or being cut off. The DIA Certified Teen Driver <u>does not cross the solid white line</u>.

The teen driver is usually caught off guard and not detecting possible conflicts at on-ramps and off-ramps and does not adjust speed and blend in. The teen driver occasionally crosses the solid white line at on ramps and off ramps.

The DIA-Certified Teen Driver, when backing out, <u>physically checks the rear of vehicle</u> prior to backing out, always taps horn, and backs up promptly and safely. The DIA-Certified Teen Driver understands the focus concept of not over-backing! The DIA- Certified Teen Driver knows to <u>back up just enough to get out safely.</u> Also, he/she understands the #1 backing rule is to eliminate backing whenever possible.

The teen driver usually gets in a vehicle and backs out, not checking rear for children or other items. The teen driver does not tap horn and has tendency to over-back.

The DIA-Certified Teen Driver understands parking lot accidents are one of most frequent accidents and focuses on (1) <u>entering at a safe speed</u>, (2) <u>scanning area</u> for backup lights and blind spots, (3) <u>communicates</u> with others who may be speeding in parking lot, (4) <u>does not over-back in parking lots</u>!

The teen driver drives at unsafe speed in parking lots, with tunnel vision, and rarely communicates with other drivers and tends to over-back.

The DIA-Certified Teen Driver drives in residential areas at posted speed limits and <u>adjusts speed according to visibility at each intersection</u>. The DIA-Certified Teen Driver constantly watches for children and/or pedestrians in front of parked vehicles. Also, he/she scans for parked vehicles with wheels turned out, or drivers in driver's seat possibly getting ready to pull out.

The teen driver at times drives too fast in residential areas and is not always looking for the hidden children in front of parked vehicles.

The DIA-Certified Teen Driver avoids following large vehicles carrying machinery (i.e., heavy equipment, landscaping trailers, flat beds carrying forklifts, or pipes) whenever possible and attempts to pass or changes lane to avoid following these vehicles as soon as possible.

The teen driver is not always aware of these situations when following large trailers with heavy equipment. There have been many accidents where an object fell off a trailer, killing or seriously injuring the occupants following behind!

The DIA-Certified Teen Driver activates night vision by looking for cars without lights. The DIA-Certified Teen Driver understands the focus concept of "in-and-out" night vision when pulling out at intersections at night. Also, he/she uses the "Minus 5. Minus 10 MPH" focus concept when driving in minimal-light situations. The DIA-Certified Teen Driver understands continuing to "activate night vision" focus concept throughout driving mission, looking for pedestrians and bicyclists until reaching the final destination.

The teen driver is usually just driving without really focusing on any objects not giving off a reflection. Reducing speed control is not a priority or habit. The teen driver is not aware of "in-and-out night vision" focus concept. The teen driver is usually surprised by pedestrians at night and does not activate night vision!

The DIA-Certified Teen Driver's goal is to not become the secondary person involved in an accident, by being a good detector. If someone runs a red light, the DIA-Certified Teen Driver would be expecting this. The DIA-Certified Teen Driver "drives like a surgeon" by being 100 percent focused and in control from point A to point B.

The teen driver usually drives with many other thoughts and habits and is easily distracted from being focused on the road 100 percent from point A to point B. This driver is a possible statistic waiting to happen!

The Bottom Line

Here's the deal: your daily mission is your survival in the most dangerous place in the world—the public highways.

Now you have received a new knowledge.

Execute with discipline all the focus concepts you have learned.

Be an In-Control driver from Point A to Point B on every driving mission.

Drive like a surgeon.

Detect and expect like the lion in the jungle. Never ever become complacent!

Help us reach target zero, one driver at a time. Your family and friends are counting on you! **Share your new knowledge with them.**

Congratulations! You are now a DIA-Certified Teen Driver.

Remember, you are about to enter the most dangerous place in the world!

Safe driving!

The Bottom Line

- <u>Here's the deal</u>: YOUR DAILY MISSION IS YOUR SURVIVAL <u>in the most dangerous place in the world—the public highways!</u>
- Now, you have received a <u>new knowledge</u>.
- EXECUTE WITH DISCIPLINE ALL THE FOCUS CONCEPTS YOU HAVE LEARNED AND BE A 100-PERCENTER!
- Be a <u>focused DIA 100 percent In-Control driver from Point A to Point B!</u>
- <u>Never ever become complacent.</u>
- Help us reach TARGET ZERO, one driver at a time! Your family and friends are counting on you.
- **We can repair your vehicle and replace the property, <u>but we cannot replace you</u>!**

Congratulations!
You are now a DIA-Certified Teen Driver!

Driving Institute of America's curriculum is based on preventative, fundamental focus concepts and is not liable for any action or inaction of anyone who is driving in various situations that may arise. As a person behind the wheel, you have a goal to follow all measures that will help prevent any accident ahead of time by being proactive and defensive based on this preventative curriculum. Safe driving!

DIA Fundamental Focus Concepts Glossary

Copyright 2013

Activate your night vision

Adjust mirrors <u>out</u> to minimize your rear blind spots and <u>use all three mirrors together</u>

Analyze your area

Avoid being rear-ended by protecting your space by controlling the vehicle behind you

Avoid abrupt lane changes and abrupt stops

Avoid blind-side pullouts

Be a disciplined 1520 driver (the solution for eliminating speeding)

Be like the lion in the jungle, and detect and expect!

Be 100 percent focused and in control from point A to point B (ultimate driving mission)

Be a 100-Percenter

Be prepared for the wrong-way driver!

Be proactive versus reactive

Be a warning sign scanner

Be well rested

Before pulling out, JUDGE the speed of cross traffic

Blend in (at on-ramps and off-ramps)

Complacency is the DANGER word! Eliminate it!

Continual-Cruising Eggshell (don't crack the eggshell)

Curves and hills reduce visibility, so reduce speed accordingly

DangerZones

Definition of a DIA-Certified Teen Driver—one who is 100 percent disciplined in following and executing all the DIA focus concepts every day for the rest of one's life. We are still a work in progress! NEVER BECOME COMPLACENT!

Detect and Expect

DIA formula for possible disaster: EXCESSIVE SPEED + WATER + CURVES AND HILLS = POSSIBLE DISASTER!

DIA five-point left-right-left-right-left scan when pulling out

DIA Pre-drive Vehicle Inspection

DIA Pre-drive Check and Setup Routine (the solution for eliminating in-vehicle distractions)

DISCIPLINE is the SAFE word

Don't be hasty when pulling out at intersections.

Don't be a blind-spot driver

Don't be looking down, TEXTING, or looking at any passengers when the wheels are rolling!

Do not OVER-BACK (minimize backing distance)

Do not rely on your mirrors alone—left or right shoulder checks when changing lanes

Drive like a surgeon—100 percent focused!

Eliminate ABRUPT lane changes

Eliminate horn blasts and skids (by being a good detector)

Eliminate in-vehicle distractions!

Go—proceeding with caution on green lights

Groupies (a group of vehicles all grouped together traveling at high speed)

Have a strategic lane driving plan

Horn is free to use—not using it can be expensive

In-and-out night vision (proper vision scan when pulling out of intersections at night)

Look for cars without lights (when pulling out of intersections at night)

Know all your lane endings and lane merges

Minimize your blind spot/Don't be a blind-spot driver

Minus 5, Minus 10 MPH (reduce mph in inclement weather and night driving)

Never turn your wheels until you are ready to execute the turn (on left turns)

On-ramps and off-ramps focus concepts—"detect and expect" and "blend in"

Physically check rear (when backing up)

Preplan all lane changes

PRESET all your music, secure your items in vehicle, and stay organized!

Protect your eggshell continually—don't crack the eggshell!

Protect your space by controlling the traffic behind you when slowing down (to avoid being rear-ended)

Reduce your speed according to visibility

Sharp blind curves—stay in your lane!

Sharp blind curves—tap your horn prior to entering curve

Staggered—being offset to have a lane opening to one or multiple lanes

Stay away from the groupies (proper space control when following cars all close together)

Strategic Lane Driving Plan—a lane driving plan to minimize lane changes and execute a safe drive until your destination

The complacent/aggressive driver IS NOT a disciplined driver and is a possible future STATISTIC!

Two major root causes of auto accidents—Distractions and Speeding

When the wheels are rolling, you can't be looking down, TEXTING, or looking at any passengers!

DIA Teen Driver
DangerZone Roadtest, TM Pending

The mission of the DIA Teen Driver parent/guardian is to analyze the first five driving routes you have planned for your teen. These routes will be the ones in your neighborhood and those they will need to drive once certified with their license. We need you to review alternate routes from home to school; you want to look at which will be the safer option based on available visibility. Are there many hills and curves, higher-speed and higher-volume highways, a route that requires too many left turns, less controlled versus uncontrolled intersections, divided versus undivided highways, and lots of pedestrians and bicyclists? You want to take the route that has fewer blind spots, the one with fewer curves and hills, less traffic, lower speed limits, fewer left turns to make, and the one with more controlled intersections versus uncontrolled intersections. Determine what you both feel is the safer route and why.

You will learn to have a strategic lane driving plan for each route, one that minimizes lane changes and conflicts. It is very important that you and your teen learn all the lane endings and lane merges of these first five routes you will be driving on. Again DIA suggests the first six months after your teen turns 16, the parent should drive these first live routes, giving a commentary while driving, and know all the DangerZones of each route. After the sixth month, then your teen begins to drive these same routes with you in the passenger seat. DIA would rather you start at 16 1/2, and teen starts driving these routes at age 17, although this is your decision based on your judgment, knowing your teen's maturity level and having a complete understanding of all you both have reviewed pertaining to these first five routes.

Prior to taking off, you will discuss your Strategic Lane Driving Plan for each route. Also complete the DIA Pre-Drive Check and Setup Routine. This will help your teen to be organized and eliminate any distractions while the wheels are rolling. Check GPS before you leave and avoid checking while vehicle is in motion. If you need to check a map or GPS, pull over to a safe area. Being disciplined is the focus concept—do not forget this!

These road tests will teach the importance of being a 100-percenter in signaling, eliminating distractions, and proper speed control according to available visibility and weather conditions at all times. Remember, you are "the second pair of eyes" during these Roadtests, so always keep an eye on the road and surroundings.

Note: Use hash marks for # of occurrences. The major items are emphasized in **bold**.

- There is DIA-Certified Teen Driver's DangerZone Roadtest Knowledge and Review that needs to be completed after doing initial DangerZone Roadtest. This will help in the retention and knowledge of the teen driver along with you the trainer.

NOTE: REVIEW ROADTEST FORM COMPLETELY TOGETHER BEFORE EACH DRIVE.

Day:_____ Date:_____ Start:_____ End:_____
ROUTE #_____ FROM:_____ TO:_____

PRE-DRIVE CHECK AND SETUP ROUTINE: CHECK OFF

CHECK TIRES AND VEHICLE CONDITION   _____
CHECK GAUGES AND SIGNAL LIGHTS   _____
MIRRORS ADJUSTED FOR OPTIMUM VISIBILITY   _____
ALL IN-VEH. NEEDS SET? RADIO/MP3/IPOD   _____
CELLPHONE—ALL ITEMS SECURED PROPERLY?   _____
ALL PERSONAL ITEMS COMPLETED (MAKEUP)   _____
STRATEGIC LANE DRIVING PLAN REVIEWED?   _____
SEAT BELT FASTENED?   _____
STRATEGIC LANE DRIVING PLAN: **Y/N** _____   **1520 PLANNED?** _____
WRITE DOWN YOU STRATEGIC LANE PLAN TO YOUR DESTINATION
(INCLUDE REASONS FOR YOUR PLAN)

_____
_____
_____
_____
_____
_____

DEPARTURE: CHECK MARK OR X FOR NOT COMPLETED

IS BACKING ABSOLUTELY NECESSARY?   _____
CLEAR AREA—PHYSICALLY CHECKED REAR   _____
CHECK MIRROR AND TAPPED HORN   _____
BACKED IMMEDIATELY AND SLOWLY?   _____
BACKING DISTANCE MINIMIZED?   _____

ON-ROAD OBSERVATION: USE HASHMARKS
LANE CHANGES   # TIMES SIGNALED % COMPLIANCE

GRADUAL/PREPLANNED LANE CHANGES

ABRUPT LANE CHANGES

LEFT TURNS MADE

REVIEWED WHEELS NOT TURNED? Y/N

INTO CORRECT LANE

SLOW DOWNS

MIRROR CHECKS

BLIND-SPOT DRIVING. # OCCURRENCES:
- CORRECT BLIND-SPOT DRIIVNG IMMEDIATELY DURING ROADTEST—FOCUS CONCEPT IS TO BE STAGGERED/OFFSET FOR VISIBILITY IN OTHER DRIVERS' MIRRORS.
- **LOW VISIBILITY AREAS** OR INTERSECTIONS (ADJUST SPEED ACCORDINGLY?)
- _____
  _____
  _____
- **HASTY PULLOUTS** AT INTERSECTIONS (HASH MARKS FOR OCCURRENCES)
- _____
  _____
- **CURVES AND HILLS (IS TEEN ADJUSTING SPEED TO REDUCED VISIBILITY?)**
- _____
  _____
  _____
  _____

- DIA-Certified Teen Driver DangerZone Roadtest – Page 3
- **STEERING CONTROL**:
- WERE HANDS IN PROPER POSITION ON TWO-LANE AND ON CURVED ROADS?
- COMMENTS: _____
- DID TEEN LOOK AT YOU WHILE THE WHEELS WERE ROLLING? Y/N
  *(ABSOLUTELY NOT TO LOOK AT YOU AS WHEELS ARE ROLLING!)   #
  OCCURRENCES: _____

- DID TEEN KNOW ALL **LANE ENDINGS**? AND ***LANE MERGES**?
- _____
  _____

- DID YOU REVIEW ALL THE PLANNED LANE STRATEGIES AFTER COMPLETING
  ROADTEST? (FOR NEXT DRIVE!)
- _____
  _____

- DID TEEN **PROTECT SPACE** BY CONTROLLING VEHICLE BEHIND?
- _____
  _____

- DID TEEN STAY AWAY FROM THE GROUPIES ON HIGH-SPEED ROADS?
- HOW WAS SPEED CONTROL?
- _____
  _____

- WHERE THERE ANY **IN-VEHICLE DISTRACTIONS** DURING THIS OBSERVATION?
- _____
  _____

- IF SO, HOW CAN THESE BE ELIMINATED IN THE FUTURE?
- _____
  _____

- WHAT **WARNING SIGNS** WERE OBSERVED AND REVIEWED? **LANE MERGES**?
- _____
  _____
  _____

- **<u>NIGHT DRIVING</u>**:
- <u>ACTIVATING NIGHT VISION REVIEWED</u>: Y/N
- <u>IN-AND-OUT NIGHT VISION EXECUTED? # OF TIMES:</u>
- Focus concept to remember: When the wheels are rolling, you can't be looking down, texting, or looking at your passengers!

AREAS TO REVIEW: Highlight Strong Points and Areas Needing Improvement

_____
_____
_____
_____
_____
_____
_____
_____
_____
_____
_____
_____
_____
_____
_____
_____
_____
_____
_____
_____
_____
_____
_____
_____
_____
_____
_____

DIA-Certified Teen Driver's Dangerzone Roadtest Knowledge And Review

Driving Institute of America® 2017

Recommend reviewing before and after going on DIA DangerZone Roadtest with your teen. Answer key is located in workbook.

1. Are you a complacent driver? _____ What type of driver will you be? A focused and In-_____ driver from Point_____ to Point _____.
    What is the 1520 rule? _____

2. The two major root causes of accidents are
    _____ and _____.

3. What is the present condition of tires, brakes, backup lights, signal lights, brake lights, wipers, and mirrors? _____

4. How disciplined is your Pre-drive Check and Setup Routine?
    Explain. _____

5. How should you adjust mirrors, and what is your goal for mirror adjustment?
    _____out and minimize my _____

6. What percentage must you tap horn when backing out? ___ percent. You should _____ check rear first? What percentage? ___. What is the main cause for backing accidents? _____.

7. What pullouts at stop signs and traffic lights are very dangerous? _____ pullouts
    What must you do prior to pulling out at stop signs and traffic lights regarding any cross traffic? _____ their speed.

8. Are you taking an extra second, or seconds, to judge the speed of cross traffic? _____

9. What must you do before making a lane change? ____plan and always avoid making any _____lane changes.

10. What is the focus concept for proper lane change?
    Preplan lane change with intent, and slide in _____

11. What does the word staggered mean? _____
    If you are not staggered, what would you be? Either in someone's _____ or _____ in.

12. When the wheels are rolling, <u>you must not be looking</u> _____, TEXTING, or looking at any_____.

13. What is your mission when driving? To be _____ percent in control from _____ to _____.

14. When approaching curves and hills, your _____ is reduced, so you must do what? _____ your speed.

15. What are two examples of low-visibility areas?
    _____ and_____

16. When approaching on-ramps and off-ramps, this is your "_____and expect" focus-concept moment.

17. The focus concept when approaching on ramps and off ramps is to _____ in properly.

18. When stopped and preparing to turn left, you must NOT have _____ turned!

19. How is your space protection? How do you protect the space in front of your vehicle?
    By _____ the vehicle behind me. This prevents what type of accident?
    Being _____-ended.

20. Are you staying away from the groupies? How do you do this? The Continual-Cruising _____.
    Who are the Groupies? Vehicles all_____ together!

21. When driving with others in vehicle, are you looking at them when you talk? _____
    Your mission is to _____on the road!

22. Speed control on curves and hills—what should you do? _____ your _____.
    Why?
    Your visibility is _____.

23. The critical first phase of the teen driver lasts _____ years.

24. The most dangerous driver is the _____ driver.

25. When driving at night you must go in AYNV mode which means "_____ your night vision."

26. When driving at night, stopped at a stop sign, and preparing to pull out, you must look for cars _____ lights!

27. Explain what in-and-out night vision is.

_____

_____

_____

28. When entering parking lots, you must _____ area, maintain a _____ speed, and _____ as needed.

29. DIA wants you to drive like a _____ and detect and _____ like the ____ in the jungle.

30. The two major behavioral root causes of accidents are _____ and _____.

31. The solutions to these root causes are (1) DIA Pre-drive Check and Setup Routine to eliminate all _____, and be a disciplined _____, which eliminates _____.

32. A green light means GO, _____with caution.

33. Left turns must be made _____, not _____ or wide.

34. Going over an overpass/bridge on a divided highway at night, being in the left lane could possibly have a _____ driver in this lane also!

DangerZone Roadtest Knowledge Review completed by:

_____ DIA-Certified Teen Driver Signature
_____ Printed Name of DIA-Certified Teen Driver
Verified by: _____ Parent Signature
_____ Printed Name of Parent
DATE: _____

Dia-Certified Teen Driver's Dangerzone Roadtest Knowledge And Review (Answer Key)

Driving Institute of America®, 2017

Recommend reviewing before and after going on Roadtest with your teen. Answer key is located in workbook.

1. Are you a complacent driver? <u>NO</u> What type of driver will you be? A focused and in-<u>CONTROL</u> driver from point <u>A</u> to point <u>B</u>
    What is the 1520 rule? <u>PLAN ARRIVAL TO DESTINATION 15–20 MIN. SOONER.</u>

2. The two major root causes of accidents are
    <u>DISTRACTIONS</u> and <u>SPEEDING</u>.

3. What is the present condition of tires, brakes, backup lights, signal lights, brake lights, wipers, and mirrors? <u>ALL OPERABLE</u>

4. How disciplined is your Pre-drive Check and Setup Routine?
    Explain <u>PRESET ALL MUSIC, SECURE ALL ITEMS AND BE ORGANIZED</u>

5. How should you adjust mirrors, and what is your goal for mirror adjustment? <u>ADJUST</u> out and minimize my <u>BLIND SPOT</u>

6. What percentage must you tap horn when backing out? <u>100</u> percent. You should <u>PHYSICALLY</u> check rear first? What percentage? <u>100</u> percent. What is main cause for backing accidents? <u>OVER-BACKING</u>.

7. What pullouts at stop signs and traffic lights are very dangerous? <u>HASTY</u> pullouts
    What must you do prior to pulling out at stop signs and traffic lights regarding any cross traffic? <u>JUDGE</u> their speed.

8. Are you taking the extra second, or seconds to judge the speed of cross traffic? <u>YES</u>

9. What must you do before making a lane change? <u>PRE</u>plan and always avoid making any <u>ABRUPT</u> lane changes.

10. What is the focus concept for proper lane change?
Preplan lane change with intent, and slide in <u>GRADUALLY</u>.

11. What does the word staggered mean? <u>OFFSET WITH AN OPENING TO ANOTHER LANE</u>
If you are not staggered, what would you be? Either in someone's <u>BLIND SPOT</u>, or <u>BOXED</u> in.

12. When the wheels are rolling, you must not be looking <u>DOWN</u>, TEXTING, or looking at any <u>PASSENGERS</u>.

13. What is your mission when driving? To be <u>100</u> percent in control from <u>POINT A</u> to <u>POINT B</u>.

14. When approaching curves and hills your <u>VISIBILITY</u> is reduced, so you must do what? <u>REDUCE</u> your speed.

15. What are two examples of low visibility areas?
<u>CURVES</u> and <u>HILLS</u>

16. When approaching on-ramps and off-ramps, this is your and "<u>DETECT</u> and expect" focus-concept moment.

17. The focus concept when approaching on-ramps and off-ramps is to <u>BLEND</u> in properly.

18. When stopped and preparing to turn left, you must NOT have <u>WHEELS</u> turned!

19. How is your space protection? How do you protect the space in front of your vehicle? By <u>CONTROLLING</u> the vehicle behind me. This prevents what type of accident? Being <u>REAR</u>-ended.

20. Are you staying away from the groupies? How do you do this? The Continual-Cruising <u>EGGSHELL</u>. Who are the groupies? Vehicles all <u>VERY CLOSE</u> together!

21. When driving with others in vehicle, are you looking at them when you talk? <u>NO</u> Your mission is to <u>FOCUS</u> on the road!

22. Speed control on curves and hills—what should you do? <u>REDUCE</u> your SPEED. Why?
Your visibility is <u>REDUCED</u>.

23. The critical first phase of the teen driver lasts <u>5</u> years.

24. The most dangerous driver is the <u>COMPLACENT</u> driver.

25. When driving at night you must go in AYNV mode which means "<u>ACTIVATE</u> your night vision."

26. When driving at night, stopped at a stop sign, and preparing to pull out, you must look for cars <u>WITHOUT</u> lights!

27. Explain what in-and-out night vision is.
<u>PRIOR TO PULLING OUT AT NIGHT, SCAN IN, THEN OUT FOR CARS WITHOUT LIGHTS ON!</u>

28. When entering parking lots, you must <u>SCAN</u> area, maintain a <u>SAFE</u> speed, and <u>COMMUNICATE</u> as needed.

29. DIA wants you to drive like a <u>SURGEON</u> and detect and <u>EXPECT</u> like the <u>LION</u> in the jungle.

30. The two major behavioral root causes of accidents are <u>DISTRACTIONS</u> and <u>SPEEDING</u>.

31. The solutions to these root causes are (1) DIA Pre-drive Check and Setup Routine to eliminate all <u>DISTRACTIONS</u>, and be a disciplined <u>1520</u> driver, which eliminates SPEEDING.

32. A green light means GO, <u>PROCEEDING</u> with caution.

33. Left turns must be made <u>SQUARE</u>, not <u>SHARP</u> or wide.

34. Going over an overpass/bridge on a divided highway at night, being in the left lane could possibly have a <u>WRONG WAY</u> driver in this lane also!

_____ DIA-Certified Teen Driver Signature
_____ Printed Name of DIA-Certified Teen Driver
Verified by: _____ Parent Signature
_____ Printed Name of Parent
DATE:_____

About the Author

The author retired after working over thirty-nine years in the transportation field. He trained frontline employees in the daily delivery and pickup process with the two largest transportation companies in the world. He specialized in defensive-driver training and amassed over 200,000 miles of observation with hundreds of couriers during his tenure. He also drove over 500,000 miles himself, experiencing several situations where he could have easily been seriously hurt or killed! He has written articles and newsletters to help get this important message out to everyone who drives every single day. There are approximately 210 million drivers in the USA, and he feels everyone needs to be retrained with his fundamental focus-concept driver training. He calls them good drivers, but his goal is to certify them as **DIA-Certified Teen Drivers!** There is a huge difference, which you will see this after completing this training. He states, "It is hard to get people to understand there are many accident possibilities and danger zones out there."

With all this experience and knowledge, he still believes **a DIA-Certified Teen Driver** is one who is 100 percent disciplined in following and executing all the DIA focus concepts every day for the rest of their life. Until then, we are all still a work in progress! Complacency is a very dangerous word, and especially when it comes to driving. He has been obsessed to develop the absolute best Teen Driver training program available anywhere today. When you begin reading this curriculum, you will see the passion and concern he has for giving everyone who reads it a clear and new knowledge to survive on our highways.

You must understand DIA's primary goal is to help you and your teen driver survive the critical first phase of driving! The risk of serious or fatal accidents with 17- to 19-year-olds is four times higher, and for 16-year-olds, it is eight times higher than other drivers! From 2000 to 2017, we have lost 73,545 teens in auto accidents! This must be fixed! He wants the parent to set a great example and become the secondary trainer once learning this curriculum. He hopes one day, we in America will reach target zero! This is where we have zero vehicle-related fatalities one day in the USA!

These Focus Concepts were derived after much thought and research. You will quickly see how your driving mindset and habits will change and improve. This curriculum's main objective is also centered toward Preventing the Seven Most Serious Accidents. <u>The goal is not only focused on accident-proofing your teen, but seriously accident-proofing them! This curriculum is an additional supplemental driver training program and not intended to replace your state program.</u>

We want you to know that Driving Institute of America's motto is **"Here…Knowledge is Prevention!"**

CPSIA information can be obtained
at www.ICGtesting.com
Printed in the USA
JSHW011706290819
1268JS00001B/1

9 781645 690115